THIS BOOK
BELONGS TO:

_____

The
Holy Qur'an
For Kids

A Textbook for School Children
With English and Arabic Text

Juz 28: Qadd Samiullah
Surahs 58-66

Presented by Yahiya Emerick
With illustrations by Patricia Meehan

Bismillahir Rahmanir Rahim

In the Name of Allah,
The Caring and the Merciful.

The Holy Qur'an for Kids – Juz 28: Qadd Samiullah
A Textbbok for School Children with English and Arabic Text

Reading for Comprehension.
Textbooks for Today and Tomorrow.
The Islamic Arts Series

Grade Range 3-7

By Yahiya Emerick

Illustrated by Patricia Meehan

Reading for Comprehension: Textbooks for Today and Tomorrow, is a new effort to present information on Muslims and Islam in a manner which is in keeping with current educational standards.

This simplified learning text for young children is meant to be a supplementary teaching text for use in an elementary classroom. The teacher is encouraged to use this text as the basis for lessons on Islam and life in general. See our website for more educational resources.

Go to www.amirahpublishing.com for more information

Juz 28: Qadd Samiullah Chapter List

Dear Children...   9

Surah #	English Name	Arabic Name	Page #
58	The Petitioner	Al Mujādilah	15
59	The Gathering	Al Hashr	33
60	She Who is Interviewed	Al Mumtahinah	50
61	The Formations	As-Saff	64
62	The Congregation	Al Jumu'ah	73
63	The Hypocrites	Al Munāfiqūn	82
64	Varied Fortune	At-Taghābūn	92
65	Divorce	At-Talāq	103
66	Prohibition	At-Tahreem	113

Dear Children...

The Qur'an is the best book to read in all the world. What makes it so special is that it is a message from the One Who made the universe and everything in it. Imagine that! Allah cares about us so much that He gave us a guidebook to help us be the best people that we can be.

Allah sent messages like this to many prophets in the old days, but people back then lost their messages or mixed them up with old legends. That's why Allah sent more and more messages again and again. The last person to get a message from Allah was Prophet Muhammad, peace be upon him. This message is called the Qur'an.

Allah wants us to be good people and to stay away from things that will hurt us. He uses the words of the Qur'an to teach us right from wrong and to give us the good news of a beautiful world waiting for us in the Next Life.

Allah has offered a special deal to all of us: if we are good believers here in this life, then He will save us from a scary place called Hellfire and give us happiness forever in *Jennah!* When we read the Qur'an in the Arabic language, it makes our hearts feel good and we connect with the original words spoken to the Prophet Muhammad.

We should all learn how to read the Arabic Qur'an to get special rewards and blessings. If we do not know what the Arabic words mean, then we can read books like this one that tell you what the Qur'an is saying. This book offers the message of part 28 of the Qur'an in an easy to understand way.

When you get older, you can move up to the grown-up Qur'an and read the whole thing. Try to read a little bit of the Qur'an every day. It's good for you. The Prophet Muhammad said that a heart that ignores the Qur'an is like an empty house. When we read the Qur'an the angels come close and ask Allah to help us and give us blessings.

Make your heart a place filled with light and you will be satisfied in this world no matter what happens to you, good or bad. Then in the Next Life you can live in total happiness forever. But don't keep the good news of Allah only to yourself. The Prophet Muhammad said that the best people are the ones who learn the Qur'an and teach it with others.

So don't be afraid to share what you have learned. Bring the light of Allah's Good Book to all the world, and then Allah has promised that He will give you an extra special reward in *Jennah!* Ameen!

Yahiya Emerick
New York
January 2010

This is What Allah Said to His Prophet...

(Juz Qadd Samiullah Part 28 of the Holy Qur'an)

بسم الله الرحمن الرحيم

The Petitioner

58 Al Mujādilah
Middle Medinan Period

☞ Introduction

A woman named Khuwaylah bint Thalabah went to the Prophet and complained that her husband (and cousin), Auws ibn as-Samit, had divorced her using an old Arab custom in which the man swore that he had the same kind of feelings towards his wife that he had towards his mother, (a practice known as *Zihar*). In other words, he wouldn't marry his own mother, so he rejected ever living with his wife on the same grounds. In her own words she said, "By Allah, that Allah sent down the beginning of (chapter 58) with regard to me and Auws ibn as-Samit. He was my husband and had grown old and difficult. One day he came to me, and I argued with him about something.

He said, 'You are like my mother to me.' Then he went out and sat with some people. Then he came back in and wanted to spend time with me, and I said, 'No, by the One Who holds my soul! You won't have your way with me after you said what you said to me until after Allah and His Messenger make a judgment in our case.' He wanted to have his way with me anyway, but I pushed him away for he was a weak old man. Then I went to my neighbor, borrowed a cloak from her and then went to the Messenger of Allah and kept complaining to him of the ill treatment I received from Auws." (*Ahmad, Abu Dawud*)

A'ishah, who was in another room, overheard Khuwaylah and reports that she said to the Prophet, "Messenger of Allah! He spent my wealth and exhausted my youth. My womb produced abundantly for him. When I became old and unable to bear any more children, he pronounced Zihar on me! O Allah! I make my complaint to You." (*Bukhari*) The Prophet said to her, "Khuwaylah! Your cousin is an old man, so have mindfulness of Allah about him." As Khuwaylah continues the story, she said, "By Allah, before I left parts of the Qur'an were revealed about me." The Messenger of Allah felt the tension of receiving revelation, as he usually did, and then he relaxed and said to me, 'Khuwaylah! Allah has revealed something about you and your husband.' Then he recited to me (verses 1-4). Then the Prophet said to me, 'Order him to free a slave.' I replied, 'Messenger of Allah, he doesn't have any to free.' Then the Prophet told me, 'Let him fast for two months.' I said, 'By Allah, he's an old man and is unable to fast.' Then the Prophet told me, 'Let him feed sixty poor people a camel-load of dates.' I said, 'By Allah, he doesn't have any of that.' Then the Prophet said, 'We will help him with a basket of dates.' I said, 'Messenger of Allah, I will help him with another.' The Prophet then said, 'You have done a noble thing. Now go and give away the dates on his behalf and take care of your cousin.'" (*Ahmad, Abu Dawud*)

And so, Khuwaylah's husband was taken to task and shamed for what he did. Yet, the situation turned around with everyone trying to help him to atone for his sin. A woman's complaint was addressed to her satisfaction, and she received the credit of a great reward on her record of deeds. In later years, during the rule of 'Umar ibn al-Khat tab, Khuwaylah saw 'Umar walking in the streets of Medina followed by an attendant.

She approached him and boldly said, "When you were young, we used to call you 'Umayr. Then when you became older we called you 'Umar. Now we call you Commander of the Faithful!" With that she left. The attendant was amazed at her boldness and asked 'Umar how he could keep silent and listen to her speak to him like that.

'Umar replied, "If she spoke to me for the whole day, I would listen to her. Do you know who she was? Allah revealed a chapter about her, and if Allah can listen to her from the heavens, then who am I not to listen to her!"

In the Name of Allah,
the Compassionate, the Merciful

Allah has heard the appeal of (the woman) who brought her petition to you about her husband. Thus, she's bringing her case to Allah (for a resolution). Allah has heard what both sides have said, for Allah listens and observes. [1]

(So from now on), those (men) who distance themselves from their wives (by saying, "*You're no more my wife than my own mother*," must realize that their wives) can never be called the same as their mothers, for no one can be called their mothers except those who gave birth to them.

When they say such things, they're speaking foolishly and falsely, though Allah erases sins and forgives (those who repent). [2]

Those (men) who try to divorce their wives in this way, but who later want to take back what they pronounced, must free a bonded-servant before they can go back to each other again.

You're required to do that, and Allah is well-informed of everything you do. [3]

Whoever can't afford to do that must fast for two months in a row before (the couple) can be with each other again. (If even this task is too much of a hardship to be fulfilled), then he should feed sixty poor people.

That's how you can **demonstrate** your faith in Allah and His Messenger.

These are the rules set by Allah, and the faithless (who disregard these rules) will have a painful punishment. [4]

Those who oppose Allah and His Messenger will be brought low just like all those (sinners) who were brought low before them. As it is, We've sent clear verses (that already demonstrate this truth).

Those who covered over (their awareness of the truth) will have a hard punishment on the day when Allah will bring them all back to life and make them realize the meaning of what they did.

(Even though they may have forgotten their deeds,) Allah has kept track of their accounts, and Allah is a witness over all things. [5-6]

On Secret Meetings

> **Background Info... v. 7**
>
> Some of the hypocrites in Medina used to have secret meetings together in order to find ways to harass and annoy the Muslims.
>
> When a sincere believer would pass by them, they would wink at each other and make up stories that the relatives of that believer, who might have been out on patrol or traveling, had died.
>
> This bothered the Muslims greatly, and they complained to the Prophet about that. This verse was revealed to comfort them. (*Asbab ul-Nuzul*)

On the Day of Assembly, He's going to inform them about what they did. Indeed, Allah has knowledge of all things. [7]

> **Background Info... first part v. 8**
>
> This verse refers to the habit of the Jews of Medina who used to whisper and look menacingly upon any Muslim who passed by them. Many Muslims complained about this habit, for the way they were being looked at and whispered about made them feel that the Jews might attack them. The Prophet repeatedly asked the Jews to stop doing it, but they ignored his requests. (*Asbab ul-Nuzul*)

Don't you see that Allah knows everything in the heavens and on the earth?

There is no secret gathering of three without Him being the fourth or between five except that He's the sixth, and whether they be more or less, He's right there among them wherever they may be.

Haven't you noticed those who were forbidden to engage in secret talk?

Yet, they continue to do what they've been told not to do! They secretly make plans to do bad things and to be hostile and disobedient to the Messenger.

Don't Speak in Secret or Give False Meanings

When they come to you, (Muhammad,) they address you (in a kind of haughty manner) that even Allah doesn't use.

Then they think to themselves, "So why isn't Allah punishing us for what we said?"

Hellfire is enough to take care of them. They're going to burn in it – and, oh, how horrible a destination! [8]

All you who believe! When you hold secret meetings, don't discuss sin, hostility or disobedience to the Messenger.

Instead, talk about virtue and mindfulness (of Allah). Be mindful then (of Allah), to Whom you will be brought back. [9]

(All other kinds of) secret meetings are inspired by Shaytan so he can create disharmony among the believers, though he can do them no harm at all except as Allah allows. The believers should trust in Allah! [10]

Make Room for Others

All you who believe! When you're asked to make room in your **gatherings** (for others), then make room, for then Allah will make room for you.

When you're asked to rise up (to leave or to make more space), then arise, for Allah will raise by degrees those who believe among you and those who achieve deep insight. Allah is well-informed of all that you do. [11]

Give in Charity before Seeking Advice

All you who believe! Before going to ask the Messenger privately for advice, give something in charity before your consultation.

That's best for you and closer to purity. If you don't have the means (to give, then know) that Allah is forgiving and merciful. [12]

Are you afraid that you won't be able to give in charity before meeting privately with the Messenger?

Indeed, if you have to skip the charity, and Allah has forgiven you, then at least remain diligent in your prayers, practice regular charity and obey Allah and His Messenger, for Allah is well-informed of all that you do. [13]

On Choosing Friends Who are Against Allah

Haven't you noticed those people who turn (in friendship) to those with whom Allah is **angry**? They're neither fully with you nor with them, and they knowingly swear to lies. [14]

Allah has prepared a terrible punishment for them because what they're doing is evil. [15] They use their promises as a screen (to hide their deceit), and thus they turn others away from the path of Allah. A $SHAMEFUL$ punishment awaits them! [16]

Neither (the extent) of their fortune nor (the size) of their families will help them in the least against Allah. They're going to be companions of the Fire, *and that's where they're going to stay!* [17]

On the day when Allah resurrects them, they'll swear to Him (as to their innocence), even as they're swearing before you now, thinking they're fully justified.

But no! They're truly liars! [18] Shaytan has won them over and made them forget the remembrance of Allah, so they're on Shaytan's team, and Shaytan's team will surely lose! [19]

Indeed, those who oppose Allah and His Messenger will be humiliated in shame, for Allah has decreed, *"My messengers and I shall prevail."* Truly, Allah is strong and powerful. [20-21]

You won't find any people who believe in Allah and the Last Day loving those who oppose Allah and His Messenger, even if they're from among their own parents, children, siblings or other relatives.

They've had faith written upon their hearts, and they've been strengthened with a spirit from His Own Self.

He's going to admit them into gardens beneath which rivers flow, and there they get to stay! Allah will be happy with them, and they with Him. They're on Allah's team, and Allah's team will have the victory! [22]

🗨 Think About It

1. Why were verses 1-6 of this surah revealed to the Prophet? (p) Read the story and explain it in your own words in three sentences.

2. Why is it wrong to hold secret meetings to make plans against other people? What kinds of secret meetings can we have?

3. Why is it important to make room for everybody in a crowded gathering?

4. Why do you think people were asked to donate to poor people before going to talk to the Prophet? What do the people have to do if they cannot donate to the poor?

5. Why is it wrong to make friends with someone who hates Allah and tries to damage the feelings of Muslims?

Fill in the Words on the lines below.
Look at the **BOLD** words in the main text to see where they go

Words to Use

Gatherings   Demonstrate   Angry

---

1. That's how you can _____ your faith in Allah and His Messenger.

2. Haven't you noticed those people who turn (in friendship) to those with whom Allah is _____?

3. All you who believe! When you're asked to make room in your _____ (for others), then make room, for then Allah will make room for you.

Complete the Crossword Puzzle Below

(Words can be in any direction, even backwards!)

ACROSS

1. Who asked the Prophet
4. If this then Allah is the fourth
5. A bad way to divorce a wife in the story
7. This is what Allah's team will achieve
10. If no charity then be good at this
13. Bad people get it on Judgment Day
14. Room for others

DOWN

2. And His Messengers shall prevail
3. gathering
6. The good people will go in them
8. Everyone good will feel this way in the Next Life
9. He uses secrets to divide people
11. Cannot help a sinner against Allah
12. Give before seeing the Prophet

Arabic Text

بِسْمِ اللَّهِ الرَّحْمَٰنِ الرَّحِيمِ

١ قَدْ سَمِعَ اللَّهُ قَوْلَ الَّتِي تُجَادِلُكَ فِي زَوْجِهَا وَتَشْتَكِي إِلَى اللَّهِ وَاللَّهُ يَسْمَعُ تَحَاوُرَكُمَا ۚ إِنَّ اللَّهَ سَمِيعٌ بَصِيرٌ

٢ الَّذِينَ يُظَاهِرُونَ مِنْكُمْ مِنْ نِسَائِهِمْ مَا هُنَّ أُمَّهَاتِهِمْ ۖ إِنْ أُمَّهَاتُهُمْ إِلَّا اللَّائِي وَلَدْنَهُمْ ۚ وَإِنَّهُمْ لَيَقُولُونَ مُنْكَرًا مِنَ الْقَوْلِ وَزُورًا ۚ وَإِنَّ اللَّهَ لَعَفُوٌّ غَفُورٌ

٣ وَالَّذِينَ يُظَاهِرُونَ مِنْ نِسَائِهِمْ ثُمَّ يَعُودُونَ لِمَا قَالُوا فَتَحْرِيرُ رَقَبَةٍ مِنْ قَبْلِ أَنْ يَتَمَاسَّا ۚ ذَٰلِكُمْ تُوعَظُونَ بِهِ ۚ وَاللَّهُ بِمَا تَعْمَلُونَ خَبِيرٌ

٤ فَمَنْ لَمْ يَجِدْ فَصِيَامُ شَهْرَيْنِ مُتَتَابِعَيْنِ مِنْ قَبْلِ أَنْ يَتَمَاسَّا ۖ فَمَنْ لَمْ يَسْتَطِعْ فَإِطْعَامُ سِتِّينَ مِسْكِينًا ۚ ذَٰلِكَ لِتُؤْمِنُوا بِاللَّهِ وَرَسُولِهِ ۚ وَتِلْكَ حُدُودُ اللَّهِ ۗ وَلِلْكَافِرِينَ عَذَابٌ أَلِيمٌ

٥ إِنَّ الَّذِينَ يُحَادُّونَ اللَّهَ وَرَسُولَهُ كُبِتُوا كَمَا كُبِتَ الَّذِينَ مِنْ قَبْلِهِمْ ۚ وَقَدْ أَنْزَلْنَا آيَاتٍ بَيِّنَاتٍ ۚ وَلِلْكَافِرِينَ عَذَابٌ مُهِينٌ

٦ يَوْمَ يَبْعَثُهُمُ اللَّهُ جَمِيعًا فَيُنَبِّئُهُمْ بِمَا عَمِلُوا ۚ أَحْصَاهُ اللَّهُ وَنَسُوهُ ۚ وَاللَّهُ عَلَىٰ كُلِّ شَيْءٍ شَهِيدٌ

٧ أَلَمْ تَرَ أَنَّ اللَّهَ يَعْلَمُ مَا فِي السَّمَاوَاتِ وَمَا فِي الْأَرْضِ ۖ مَا يَكُونُ مِنْ نَجْوَىٰ ثَلَاثَةٍ إِلَّا هُوَ رَابِعُهُمْ وَلَا خَمْسَةٍ إِلَّا هُوَ سَادِسُهُمْ وَلَا أَدْنَىٰ مِنْ ذَٰلِكَ وَلَا أَكْثَرَ إِلَّا هُوَ مَعَهُمْ أَيْنَ مَا كَانُوا ۖ ثُمَّ يُنَبِّئُهُمْ بِمَا عَمِلُوا يَوْمَ الْقِيَامَةِ إِنَّ اللَّهَ بِكُلِّ شَيْءٍ عَلِيمٌ

٨ أَلَمْ تَرَ إِلَى الَّذِينَ نُهُوا عَنِ النَّجْوَىٰ ثُمَّ يَعُودُونَ لِمَا نُهُوا عَنْهُ وَيَتَنَاجَوْنَ بِالْإِثْمِ وَالْعُدْوَانِ وَمَعْصِيَتِ الرَّسُولِ وَإِذَا جَاءُوكَ حَيَّوْكَ بِمَا لَمْ يُحَيِّكَ بِهِ اللَّهُ وَيَقُولُونَ فِي أَنْفُسِهِمْ لَوْلَا يُعَذِّبُنَا اللَّهُ بِمَا نَقُولُ ۚ حَسْبُهُمْ جَهَنَّمُ يَصْلَوْنَهَا ۖ فَبِئْسَ الْمَصِيرُ

٩ يَا أَيُّهَا الَّذِينَ آمَنُوا إِذَا تَنَاجَيْتُمْ فَلَا تَتَنَاجَوْا بِالْإِثْمِ وَالْعُدْوَانِ وَمَعْصِيَتِ الرَّسُولِ وَتَنَاجَوْا بِالْبِرِّ وَالتَّقْوَىٰ ۖ وَاتَّقُوا اللَّهَ الَّذِي إِلَيْهِ تُحْشَرُونَ

١٠ إِنَّمَا النَّجْوَىٰ مِنَ الشَّيْطَانِ لِيَحْزُنَ الَّذِينَ آمَنُوا وَلَيْسَ بِضَارِّهِمْ شَيْئًا إِلَّا بِإِذْنِ اللَّهِ ۚ وَعَلَى اللَّهِ فَلْيَتَوَكَّلِ الْمُؤْمِنُونَ

١١ يَا أَيُّهَا الَّذِينَ آمَنُوا إِذَا قِيلَ لَكُمْ تَفَسَّحُوا فِي الْمَجَالِسِ فَافْسَحُوا يَفْسَحِ اللَّهُ لَكُمْ ۖ وَإِذَا قِيلَ انْشُزُوا فَانْشُزُوا يَرْفَعِ اللَّهُ الَّذِينَ آمَنُوا مِنْكُمْ وَالَّذِينَ أُوتُوا الْعِلْمَ دَرَجَاتٍ ۚ وَاللَّهُ بِمَا تَعْمَلُونَ خَبِيرٌ

١٢ يَا أَيُّهَا الَّذِينَ آمَنُوا إِذَا نَاجَيْتُمُ الرَّسُولَ فَقَدِّمُوا بَيْنَ يَدَيْ نَجْوَاكُمْ صَدَقَةً ۚ ذَٰلِكَ خَيْرٌ لَكُمْ وَأَطْهَرُ ۚ فَإِنْ لَمْ تَجِدُوا فَإِنَّ اللَّهَ غَفُورٌ رَحِيمٌ

١٣ أَأَشْفَقْتُمْ أَنْ تُقَدِّمُوا بَيْنَ يَدَيْ نَجْوَاكُمْ صَدَقَاتٍ ۚ فَإِذْ لَمْ تَفْعَلُوا وَتَابَ اللَّهُ عَلَيْكُمْ فَأَقِيمُوا الصَّلَاةَ وَآتُوا الزَّكَاةَ وَأَطِيعُوا اللَّهَ وَرَسُولَهُ ۚ وَاللَّهُ خَبِيرٌ بِمَا تَعْمَلُونَ

١٤ أَلَمْ تَرَ إِلَى الَّذِينَ تَوَلَّوْا قَوْمًا غَضِبَ اللَّهُ عَلَيْهِمْ مَا هُمْ مِنْكُمْ وَلَا مِنْهُمْ وَيَحْلِفُونَ عَلَى الْكَذِبِ وَهُمْ يَعْلَمُونَ

١٥ أَعَدَّ اللَّهُ لَهُمْ عَذَابًا شَدِيدًا ۖ إِنَّهُمْ سَاءَ مَا كَانُوا يَعْمَلُونَ

١٦ اتَّخَذُوا أَيْمَانَهُمْ جُنَّةً فَصَدُّوا عَنْ سَبِيلِ اللَّهِ فَلَهُمْ عَذَابٌ مُهِينٌ

١٧ لَنْ تُغْنِيَ عَنْهُمْ أَمْوَالُهُمْ وَلَا أَوْلَادُهُمْ مِنَ اللَّهِ شَيْئًا ۚ أُولَٰئِكَ أَصْحَابُ النَّارِ ۖ هُمْ فِيهَا خَالِدُونَ

١٨ يَوْمَ يَبْعَثُهُمُ اللَّهُ جَمِيعًا فَيَحْلِفُونَ لَهُ كَمَا يَحْلِفُونَ لَكُمْ ۖ وَيَحْسَبُونَ أَنَّهُمْ عَلَىٰ شَيْءٍ ۚ أَلَا إِنَّهُمْ هُمُ الْكَاذِبُونَ

١٩ اسْتَحْوَذَ عَلَيْهِمُ الشَّيْطَانُ فَأَنْسَاهُمْ ذِكْرَ اللَّهِ ۚ أُولَٰئِكَ حِزْبُ الشَّيْطَانِ ۚ أَلَا إِنَّ حِزْبَ الشَّيْطَانِ هُمُ الْخَاسِرُونَ

٢٠ إِنَّ الَّذِينَ يُحَادُّونَ اللَّهَ وَرَسُولَهُ أُولَٰئِكَ فِي الْأَذَلِّينَ

٢١ كَتَبَ اللَّهُ لَأَغْلِبَنَّ أَنَا وَرُسُلِي ۚ إِنَّ اللَّهَ قَوِيٌّ عَزِيزٌ

26

٢٢ لَا تَجِدُ قَوْمًا يُؤْمِنُونَ بِاللَّهِ وَالْيَوْمِ الْآخِرِ يُوَادُّونَ مَنْ حَادَّ اللَّهَ وَرَسُولَهُ وَلَوْ كَانُوا آبَاءَهُمْ أَوْ أَبْنَاءَهُمْ أَوْ إِخْوَانَهُمْ أَوْ عَشِيرَتَهُمْ ۚ أُولَٰئِكَ كَتَبَ فِي قُلُوبِهِمُ الْإِيمَانَ وَأَيَّدَهُمْ بِرُوحٍ مِنْهُ ۖ وَيُدْخِلُهُمْ جَنَّاتٍ تَجْرِي مِنْ تَحْتِهَا الْأَنْهَارُ خَالِدِينَ فِيهَا ۚ رَضِيَ اللَّهُ عَنْهُمْ وَرَضُوا عَنْهُ ۚ أُولَٰئِكَ حِزْبُ اللَّهِ ۚ أَلَا إِنَّ حِزْبَ اللَّهِ هُمُ الْمُفْلِحُونَ

Surah 58 Transliteration

Bismillahir Rahmanir Rahim

1. Qad sami'al laahu qawlal latee tujaadiluka fee zawjihaa wa tashtakee ilallaahi wallaahu yasma'u tahaa wurakumaa; innallaaha samee'um baseer

2. Allazeena yuzaahiroona minkum min nisaa'ihim maa hunnaa ummahaatihim. In ummahaatuhum illal laa-ee walad nahum; wa innaahum la yaqooloona munkaram minal qawli wa zooraa; wa innallaaha la'afuwwun ghafoor

3. Wallazeena yuzaahiroona min nisaa'ihim thumma ya'oodoona limaa qaaloo fatahreeru raqabatim min qabli ay-yatamaassaa; zaalikum too'azoona bih; wallaahu bimaa ta'maloona khabeer

4. Famal lam yajid fa siyaamu shahrayni mutataabi'ayni min qabli ay-yatamaa ssaa famal lam yastati' fa-it'aamu sitteena miskeena; zaalika litu-minoo billaahi wa rasoolih. Wa tilka hudoodul laah; wa lilkaafireena 'azaabun aleem

5. Innal lazeena yuhaaddoonal laaha wa Rasoolahoo kubitoo kamaa kubital lazeena min qablihim; wa qad anzalnaa aayaatim baiyinaat; wa lilkaa fireena 'azaabum muheen

6. Yawma yab'athuhumullaahu jamee'an fayunabbi'uhum bimaa 'amiloo; ahsaahul laahu wa nasooh; wallaahu 'alaa kulli shay'in shaheed

7. Alam tara annallaaha ya'lamu maa fis samaawaati wa maa fil 'ard. Maa yakoonu min najwaa salaasatin illaa Huwa raabi'uhum wa laa khamsatin illaa huwa saadisuhum wa laa adnaa min zaalika wa laa akthara illaa huwa ma'ahum ayna maa kaanoo thumma yunabbi'uhum bimaa 'amiloo yawmal qiyaamah; innal laaha bikulli shay'in aleem

8. Alam tara ilal lazeena nuhoo 'anin najwaa thumma ya'oodoona limaa nuhoo 'anhu wa yatanaajawna bil ithmi wal'udwaani wa ma'siyatir rasooli wa izaa jaa'ooka haiyawka bimaa lam yuhai yika bihil laahu wa yaqooloona fee anfusihim law laa yu'azzibunal laahu bimaa naqool; hasbuhum jahannnamu yaslawnahaa fabi-sal maseer

29

9. Yaa ayyuhal lazeena aamanoo izaa tanaajaytum falaa tatanaajaw bil ithmi wal 'udwaani wa ma'siyatir rasooli wa tanaajaw bil birri wattaqwaa wattaqul laahal lazee ilayhi tuhsharoon

10. Innaman najwaa minash shaytaani liyahzunal lazeena aamanoo wa laysa bidaarrihim shay'an illaa bi-iznillaah; wa 'alallaahi falyatawakkalil mu'minoon

11. Yaa ayyuhal lazeena aamanoo izaa qeela lakum tafassahoo fil majaalisi fafsahoo yafsahil laahu lakum wa izaa qeelan shuzoo fanshuzoo yarfa'il laahul lazeena aamanoo minkum wallazeena ootul 'ilma darajaat; wallaahu bimaa ta'maloona khabeer

12. Yaa ayyuhal lazeena aamanoo izaa naajaytumur Rasoola faqaddimoo bayna yadai najwaakum sadaqah; zaalika khairul lakum wa athar; fa il lam tajidoo fa innal laaha ghafoorur Raheem

13. 'A-ashfaqtum an tuqaddimoo bayna yaday najwaakum sadaqaat; fa-iz lam taf'aloo wa taabal laahu 'alaikum fa aqeemus Salaata wa aatuz Zakaata wa atee'ul laaha wa rasoolah; wallaahu khabeerum bimaa ta'maloon

14. Alam tara ilal lazeena tawallaw qawman ghadibal laahu 'alayhim maa hum minkum wa laa minhum wa yahlifoona 'alal kazibi wa hum ya'lamoon

15. A'addal laahu lahum 'azaaban shadeedan innahum saa-a maa kaanoo ya'maloon

16. It takhazoo aymaanahum junnatan fasaddoo 'an sabeelil laahi falahum 'azaabum muheen

17. Lan tughniya 'anhum amwaaluhum wa laa awladuhum minal laahi shay-aa; ulaa-ika as haabun Naari hum feehaa khaalidoon

18. Yawma yab'asuhumul laahujamee'an fa yahlifoona lahoo kamaa yahlifoona lakum wa yah saboona annahum 'alaa shay; alaa innahum humul kaaziboon

19. Istahwaza 'alayhimush shaytaanu fa ansaahum zikral laah; ulaa-ika hizbush shaytaan; alaa innaa hizbash shaytaani humul khaasiroon

20. Innal lazeena yuhaaddoonal laaha wa Rasoolahoo ulaa-ika fil azalleen

21. Katabal laahu la aghlibanna ana wa Rusulee; innal laaha qawiyyun 'Azeez

22.	Laa tajidu qawmaiy yu'minoona billaahi wal yawmil aakhiri yuwaad doona man haad dal laaha wa Rasoolahoo wa law kaanoo aabaa'ahum aw abnaa'ahum aw ikhwaa nahum aw 'asheeratahum; ulaa-ika kataba fee quloobihi mul emaana wa ayyadahum biroohim minhu wa yudkhilu hum jannatin tajree min tahtihal anhaaru khaalideena feehaa; radiyal laahu 'anhum wa radoo 'anhu; ulaa 'ika hizbullah; alaa inna hizballahi humul muf lihoon

The Gathering

59 Al Hashr
Early Medinan Period

👉 Introduction

In the year 624, an outnumbered force of Muslims defeated a Meccan army at the Wells of Badr. This elevated the status of the Muslims in the eyes of the Arabs and caused a great amount of embarrassment for the Meccans. In Medina, it also gave pause for the three Jewish tribes to reconsider Muhammad's (p) rising power. Even though each had signed a city charter with him guaranteeing the mutual safety of all, none of them had considered Muhammad (p) or his religion to be a permanent fixture in Arabia.

The tribe of Banu Qaynuqa decided to scrap the treaty first, and they challenged the Muslims to a fight, but they were defeated and banished from the city. Meanwhile, among the Banu Nadir there were those who were impressed with the Muslim victory at Badr. A few even took it as a sign that Muhammad might just be a true prophet, and a few of those even converted to Islam, given that he apparently had the favor of Allah. However, the majority of the tribe were content to remain quietly opposed in their attitude.

The angry Meccans soon began to send messages to the Banu Nadir, one of which said, "You're the people who have fortresses and military might. You had better fight the Prophet, otherwise we'll attack (him and then you), and nothing will prevent us from seizing your women." This only added to the internal debate among the Banu Nadir about what to do about Islam.

After the Muslims were defeated by the Meccans the following year at the Battle of Uhud (in the year 625), the leaders among the Banu Nadir felt that this showed that Muhammad (p) did not have the favor of Allah after all. Thus, they increased in their quiet resistance to Islam. A delegation of forty men led by a chief of the Banu Nadir, Ka'b ibn Ashraf, traveled to Mecca and pledged support to the pagans in their fight against Islam.

When they retuned to Medina, they began to make secret pledges of support with some factions of hypocrites within the city, even extracting a promise from 'Abdullah ibn Ubayy that if they fought the Muslims, then Ibn Ubayy's men would back them up – and even share their fate if their side lost. (The Meccans had also written a similar threatening letter to Ibn Ubayy to force his support.)

Eventually, the Banu Nadir faction resolved to assassinate the Prophet. They asked the Prophet to come with thirty followers – and they would join him with thirty followers of their own – to hold a summit meeting. When the meeting was underway, some of the rabbis, realizing that Muhammad's (p) followers were fervent enough to fight to the death, reconsidered attacking him there.

So, one of them told Muhammad, (p) "How can we come to an agreement when we're a mass of sixty men? Come and visit us with three of your men, and we'll bring three of our good people. If any of them believe in you, at least one of us will have believed in you."

When the time for the next meeting was at hand, three Jewish men with swords awaited to ambush the Prophet. A Jewish woman of the Banu Nadir, whose own son had converted to Islam, warned her son of the plot to kill the Prophet, and he went to the Prophet right away with the news. The Prophet refrained from attending that meeting and took to avoiding the neighborhood of the Banu Nadir. It is reported that the Prophet publicly called to be 'relieved' of Ka'b ibn Ashraf and his plotting and propagandizing, and he was killed in a clandestine ambush by one of the companions a short time later.

Eventually, the Prophet would have to pay a visit to the Banu Nadir's district, and here is the background for that story. A man named 'Amr ibn Umayyah Damuri had survived a massacre in which almost seventy of the Prophet's missionaries had been ambushed and killed, despite promises of safe passage from an ostensibly sincere tribe that was secretly allied to the Meccans. On his way back to Medina with the grim news, 'Amr, who was the sole survivor, encountered two pagans and attacked them, thinking they had been involved in the massacre.

When he finally returned to the city, he found out that the two men were not a part of the ambush and that their tribe was allied to both the Muslims and the Banu Nadir. The Prophet then ordered blood-money to be collected to compensate the victims' families for the unintended loss of their two men, and he also went to pay a visit to the district of the Banu Nadir to collect money from them for the same purpose, as they were supposed to pay according to their contract.

Apparently, the men who received the Prophet and his companions asked him to sit in the shade of a wall and wait for them to meet with him. A young Jewish man named 'Umar ibn Jahash was tapped by the Jewish elders to drop a heavy stone from the roof in an attempt to kill the Prophet, but the Prophet noticed the activity from above and quickly retreated with his followers back into the Muslim district of the city. Thereupon, the Prophet called for his followers to arm themselves, and they went to the fortress complex of the Banu Nadir and besieged it.

The Prophet ordered them to leave Medina within ten days, or he would attack. The Banu Nadir sent a desperate message to 'Abdullah ibn Ubayy to reinforce them, but he remained in his own neighborhood and forsook them. (Not even their Jewish cousins, the Banu Qurayzah, came to their aid, preferring to sign a renewed mutual security agreement with Muhammad.)

The clever men of the Banu Nadir held out for about fifteen days by raining arrows down upon the Muslims to keep them away. Finally, after a spirited defense of their position, they saw the Muslims uprooting some of their precious orchards, and they quickly lost the will to fight. Eventually the pressure of the siege forced the Banu Nadir to sue for peace. Trusting in Muhammad's lenient reputation, they surrendered some days later, and he gave them quite generous terms, considering what they tried to do to him.

The tribe was ordered to leave Medina because of their betrayal of the treaty. Yet, they would have the originally ordered ten days to pack, and they could take whatever they could load onto their camels. Before they left, the Banu Nadir practically demolished their homes to keep the Muslims from enjoying them. Most of the tribe then moved to Syria, though a remnant went to a Jewish settlement named Khaybar far to the north. (From there they would later seek revenge by creating an alliance of pagans together to surround the city of Medina!)

An old Drawing of Medina from the 1700s

All things within the heavens and on the earth glorify Allah. He's the Powerful and the Wise. [1]

He's the One Who drove the faithless from among the Followers of Earlier Revelation away from their homes – even at the first gathering (for battle)!

You never thought (the Banu Nadir) would leave, even as they thought their fortresses could stand against Allah.

Then Allah came upon them from every direction and from where they least expected! He cast fear into their hearts, causing them to destroy their homes with their own hands – (even helping) the believers' efforts in the process! You who have eyes to see, take heed. [2]

If Allah had not already decreed their exile, He would've certainly imposed upon them far greater punishment in this world, though the punishment of the Fire awaits them in the next life. [3]

That's because they **opposed** Allah and His Messenger, and anyone who opposes Allah (should know) that Allah is severe in retribution. [4]

Whether you had cut the palm trees or let them stand firmly, it was all by the will of Allah, (though He commanded them to be cut) so that the rebels could be disgraced. [5]

(The property) that Allah (removed from their control) and transferred to His Messenger required no expedition of cavalry or camelry on your part, for Allah grants His messengers power over whomever He wants, for Allah has power over all things. [6]

Whatever (property) Allah transferred to His Messenger from the people of the (Banu Nadir and their) settlement belongs to Allah and His Messenger and to relatives, to orphans, to the needy and to travelers, so that the money doesn't remain circulating among the wealthy alone.

So take what the Messenger gives out for you, and refrain from what he withholds from you. Be mindful of Allah, for Allah is severe in retribution. [7]

(Also distribute something) to the poor refugees (from Mecca) who were driven from their homes and deprived of their properties in their pursuit of the grace and pleasure of Allah, and also because they were helping Allah and His Messenger. They were sincere (in their intentions). [8]

Don't be Jealous of the Fortunes of Others

> **Background Info... first part v. 9**
>
> After the Banu Nadir left Medina and headed northwards, the Prophet gave a speech about the distribution of the lands they left behind to the gathered throngs of jubilant (and expectant) believers.
>
> He told the crowd, which was made up mostly of Helpers (natives of Medina who took in the Meccan refugees), "Allah has granted you the wealth of the Banu Nadir.
>
> "If you like, I will divide the wealth among the Immigrants and Helpers equally, and the Immigrants will continue to live in the homes of the Helpers, or if you like, the wealth can be distributed among the homeless Immigrants, and they can thus move out of your homes and into their own new ones."
>
> The Helpers generously deferred all the wealth to the Immigrants, who were thus able to establish themselves in the city in their own homes. (*Ma'ariful Qur'an*)

Those who already had homes here (in Medina) and who believed (in Islam), extended their heartfelt hospitality to those (Meccan refugees) who came to them seeking a safe haven. They're not inwardly jealous of the portions (that the refugees) are receiving.

> **Background Info... Second part v. 9-10**
>
> The Prophet sent a hungry Immigrant to a Helper's house for a meal. (The Prophet had first asked his own wives if they had any food for the man, and they had nothing in their apartments except water!)
>
> The Helper who volunteered to feed the Immigrant went inside his home and asked his wife if there was any food in the house. She answered that there was only enough for the children.
>
> So he asked her to blow out the lamp in their room and put the children to bed. Then he invited the Immigrant in and fed the food to his visitor.
>
> When the Prophet heard about this, he told the Helper that the (angels) in the sky were astonished at what he had done. Then the second half of this verse along with verse ten was revealed for him. (*Bukhari, Muslim*)

And even though they might be needy themselves, they give preference to others first. Whoever is saved from the **greed** of his own soul will be successful. [9]

Those (believers) who came after them said, "*Our Lord, forgive us and our brothers (in faith) who came before us. Don't let any malice against other believers take root within our hearts, for You are, Our Lord, kind and merciful.*" [10]

An Unholy Alliance

Haven't you noticed how the hypocrites behave towards their 'brothers' among the Followers of Earlier Revelation?

(They conspired with them), saying, *"If you're banished (for breaking your treaty with the Muslims), then we'll all go into exile together. We'll never listen to anyone else ever. If war is waged against you, then we'll come to your aid."*

Allah is a witness that they're all liars, for if the (Banu Nadir) are banished, (the hypocrites) would never follow them, and if war is made, (the hypocrites) would never help them.

If a (few of them) did, then they would turn back (in cowardice) and find no one to help them themselves! [11-12]

For sure, you're stronger than they are, for their minds are afflicted with dread from Allah! That's because they're a people who lack understanding. [13]

They'll never fight you in united front, except from behind fortified areas or mighty ramparts, and even though their bravado might make it seem as if they're strong and united, in reality they're hearts are divided, for they're a people devoid of sense. [14]

They're like those nearby (Jews of the Banu Qaynuqa) who felt the results of their affair.

They're going to have a painful punishment (in the afterlife), as well. [15]

Their (friends fooled them) just like **Shaytan** does when he entices human beings, saying, "*Hide (the truth)!*"

However, as soon as someone tries to cover up (his natural belief in Allah and suffers His wrath,) Shaytan shouts, *"I'm not responsible for you. I fear Allah, the Lord of All the Worlds!"* [16]

In the end, they'll both be in the Fire, and they're going to remain within, for that's the reward of the wrongdoers. [17]

Mind Your Real Investment Returns

All you who believe! Be mindful (of Allah), and let every soul consider what it has invested for the future. Be mindful (of Allah), for Allah is well-informed of all that you do. [18]

Don't be like those who forgot about Allah, for Allah then **allowed** them to forget (what was best) for their own souls. They're truly the disobedient ones. [19]

The companions of the Fire can never be (thought of as) equal to the companions of the Garden, because only the companions of the Garden will achieve complete bliss. [20]

If We had sent this Qur'an down upon a mountain, you would've seen it humble itself and break apart for fear of Allah. These are

the kinds of examples We lay out for people, so they can use their reason. [21]

A Song of Praise

He is Allah, before Whom there are no others.

He knows what's beyond sight As well as what's plainly seen.

He's the Compassionate, the Merciful! [22]

He is Allah, before Whom there are no others:

the Master, the Holy, the Source of Peace, the Guardian of Faith, the Protector, the Powerful, the Compeller, the Majestic.

Glory be to Allah! He's far above what they attribute to Him. [23]

He is Allah, the Creator, the Evolver, the Fashioner. The most beautiful names are His.

All things within the heavens and the earth declare His praise, for He is the Powerful, and the Wise. [24]

💭 Think About It

1. After you read the introduction, explain in your own words why it was completely fair to make the Banu Nadir leave Medina and move somewhere else?

2. Verses 7-8 tell us about a basic principle of a government based on obedience to Allah. When a Muslim group gets a lot of money, why do they have to give so much of it to the poor?

3. What is a hypocrite, and why can you never trust their promises?

4. Why are verses 18-19 so important?

5. Choose one of the titles of Allah from verses 22-24. What is it, and what does it mean to you?

Fill in the Words on the lines below.
Look at the **BOLD** words in the main text to see where they go

Words to Use

Allowed   Opposed   Greed   Shaytan

---

1. That's because they _____ Allah and His Messenger, and anyone who opposes Allah (should know) that Allah is severe in retribution.

2. Their (friends fooled them) just like _____ does when he entices human beings, saying, "*Hide (the truth)!*"

3. Don't be like those who forgot about Allah, for Allah then _____ them to forget (what was best) for their own souls.

4. Whoever is saved from the _____ of his own soul will be successful.

Complete the Crossword Puzzle Below

(Words can be in any direction, even backwards!)

ACROSS

1. The Most Beautiful
3. Trees
4. The Banu Nadir were sent away
6. Comes before the Fashioner
8. The Banu Nadir broke it
10. Be this of Allah
11. They got new things
13. The Banu...
14. The Banu Nadir destroyed them out of anger
15. What lives on after death

DOWN

2. Makes false promises
5. They say one thing but do another
7. Don't be if others get more than you
9. Comes after the Compeller
10. This is where the Prophet lived
12. It can ruin your soul
14. The Fourth name of Allah in verses 22-24

Arabic Text

بسم الله الرحمن الرحيم

١ سَبَّحَ لِلَّهِ مَا فِي السَّمَاوَاتِ وَمَا فِي الْأَرْضِ ۖ وَهُوَ الْعَزِيزُ الْحَكِيمُ

٢ هُوَ الَّذِي أَخْرَجَ الَّذِينَ كَفَرُوا مِنْ أَهْلِ الْكِتَابِ مِنْ دِيَارِهِمْ لِأَوَّلِ الْحَشْرِ ۚ مَا ظَنَنْتُمْ أَنْ يَخْرُجُوا ۖ وَظَنُّوا أَنَّهُمْ مَانِعَتُهُمْ حُصُونُهُمْ مِنَ اللَّهِ فَأَتَاهُمُ اللَّهُ مِنْ حَيْثُ لَمْ يَحْتَسِبُوا ۖ وَقَذَفَ فِي قُلُوبِهِمُ الرُّعْبَ ۚ يُخْرِبُونَ بُيُوتَهُمْ بِأَيْدِيهِمْ وَأَيْدِي الْمُؤْمِنِينَ فَاعْتَبِرُوا يَا أُولِي الْأَبْصَارِ

٣ وَلَوْلَا أَنْ كَتَبَ اللَّهُ عَلَيْهِمُ الْجَلَاءَ لَعَذَّبَهُمْ فِي الدُّنْيَا ۖ وَلَهُمْ فِي الْآخِرَةِ عَذَابُ النَّارِ

٤ ذَٰلِكَ بِأَنَّهُمْ شَاقُّوا اللَّهَ وَرَسُولَهُ ۖ وَمَنْ يُشَاقِّ اللَّهَ فَإِنَّ اللَّهَ شَدِيدُ الْعِقَابِ

٥ مَا قَطَعْتُمْ مِنْ لِينَةٍ أَوْ تَرَكْتُمُوهَا قَائِمَةً عَلَىٰ أُصُولِهَا فَبِإِذْنِ اللَّهِ وَلِيُخْزِيَ الْفَاسِقِينَ

٦ وَمَا أَفَاءَ اللَّهُ عَلَىٰ رَسُولِهِ مِنْهُمْ فَمَا أَوْجَفْتُمْ عَلَيْهِ مِنْ خَيْلٍ وَلَا رِكَابٍ وَلَٰكِنَّ اللَّهَ يُسَلِّطُ رُسُلَهُ عَلَىٰ مَنْ يَشَاءُ ۚ وَاللَّهُ عَلَىٰ كُلِّ شَيْءٍ قَدِيرٌ

٧ مَا أَفَاءَ اللَّهُ عَلَىٰ رَسُولِهِ مِنْ أَهْلِ الْقُرَىٰ فَلِلَّهِ وَلِلرَّسُولِ وَلِذِي الْقُرْبَىٰ وَالْيَتَامَىٰ وَالْمَسَاكِينِ وَابْنِ السَّبِيلِ كَيْ لَا يَكُونَ دُولَةً بَيْنَ الْأَغْنِيَاءِ مِنْكُمْ ۚ وَمَا آتَاكُمُ الرَّسُولُ فَخُذُوهُ وَمَا نَهَاكُمْ عَنْهُ فَانْتَهُوا ۚ وَاتَّقُوا اللَّهَ ۖ إِنَّ اللَّهَ شَدِيدُ الْعِقَابِ

٨ لِلْفُقَرَاءِ الْمُهَاجِرِينَ الَّذِينَ أُخْرِجُوا مِنْ دِيَارِهِمْ وَأَمْوَالِهِمْ يَبْتَغُونَ فَضْلًا مِنَ اللَّهِ وَرِضْوَانًا وَيَنْصُرُونَ اللَّهَ وَرَسُولَهُ ۚ أُولَٰئِكَ هُمُ الصَّادِقُونَ

٩ وَالَّذِينَ تَبَوَّءُوا الدَّارَ وَالْإِيمَانَ مِنْ قَبْلِهِمْ يُحِبُّونَ مَنْ هَاجَرَ إِلَيْهِمْ وَلَا يَجِدُونَ فِي صُدُورِهِمْ حَاجَةً مِمَّا أُوتُوا وَيُؤْثِرُونَ عَلَىٰ أَنْفُسِهِمْ وَلَوْ كَانَ بِهِمْ خَصَاصَةٌ ۚ وَمَنْ يُوقَ شُحَّ نَفْسِهِ فَأُولَٰئِكَ هُمُ الْمُفْلِحُونَ

١٠ وَالَّذِينَ جَاءُوا مِنْ بَعْدِهِمْ يَقُولُونَ رَبَّنَا اغْفِرْ لَنَا وَلِإِخْوَانِنَا الَّذِينَ سَبَقُونَا بِالْإِيمَانِ وَلَا تَجْعَلْ فِي قُلُوبِنَا غِلًّا لِلَّذِينَ آمَنُوا رَبَّنَا إِنَّكَ رَءُوفٌ رَحِيمٌ

١١ أَلَمْ تَرَ إِلَى الَّذِينَ نَافَقُوا يَقُولُونَ لِإِخْوَانِهِمُ الَّذِينَ كَفَرُوا مِنْ أَهْلِ الْكِتَابِ لَئِنْ أُخْرِجْتُمْ لَنَخْرُجَنَّ مَعَكُمْ وَلَا نُطِيعُ فِيكُمْ أَحَدًا أَبَدًا وَإِنْ قُوتِلْتُمْ لَنَنْصُرَنَّكُمْ وَاللَّهُ يَشْهَدُ إِنَّهُمْ لَكَاذِبُونَ

١٢ لَئِنْ أُخْرِجُوا لَا يَخْرُجُونَ مَعَهُمْ وَلَئِنْ قُوتِلُوا لَا يَنْصُرُونَهُمْ وَلَئِنْ نَصَرُوهُمْ لَيُوَلُّنَّ الْأَدْبَارَ ثُمَّ لَا يُنْصَرُونَ

١٣ لَأَنْتُمْ أَشَدُّ رَهْبَةً فِي صُدُورِهِمْ مِنَ اللَّهِ ۚ ذَٰلِكَ بِأَنَّهُمْ قَوْمٌ لَا يَفْقَهُونَ

١٤ لَا يُقَاتِلُونَكُمْ جَمِيعًا إِلَّا فِي قُرًى مُحَصَّنَةٍ أَوْ مِنْ وَرَاءِ جُدُرٍ ۚ بَأْسُهُمْ بَيْنَهُمْ شَدِيدٌ ۚ تَحْسَبُهُمْ جَمِيعًا وَقُلُوبُهُمْ شَتَّىٰ ۚ ذَٰلِكَ بِأَنَّهُمْ قَوْمٌ لَا يَعْقِلُونَ

١٥ كَمَثَلِ الَّذِينَ مِنْ قَبْلِهِمْ قَرِيبًا ۖ ذَاقُوا وَبَالَ أَمْرِهِمْ وَلَهُمْ عَذَابٌ أَلِيمٌ

١٦ كَمَثَلِ الشَّيْطَانِ إِذْ قَالَ لِلْإِنْسَانِ اكْفُرْ فَلَمَّا كَفَرَ قَالَ إِنِّي بَرِيءٌ مِنْكَ إِنِّي أَخَافُ اللَّهَ رَبَّ الْعَالَمِينَ

١٧ فَكَانَ عَاقِبَتَهُمَا أَنَّهُمَا فِي النَّارِ خَالِدَيْنِ فِيهَا ۚ وَذَٰلِكَ جَزَاءُ الظَّالِمِينَ

١٨ يَا أَيُّهَا الَّذِينَ آمَنُوا اتَّقُوا اللَّهَ وَلْتَنْظُرْ نَفْسٌ مَا قَدَّمَتْ لِغَدٍ ۖ وَاتَّقُوا اللَّهَ ۚ إِنَّ اللَّهَ خَبِيرٌ بِمَا تَعْمَلُونَ

١٩ وَلَا تَكُونُوا كَالَّذِينَ نَسُوا اللَّهَ فَأَنْسَاهُمْ أَنْفُسَهُمْ ۚ أُولَٰئِكَ هُمُ الْفَاسِقُونَ

٢٠ لَا يَسْتَوِي أَصْحَابُ النَّارِ وَأَصْحَابُ الْجَنَّةِ ۚ أَصْحَابُ الْجَنَّةِ هُمُ الْفَائِزُونَ

٢١ لَوْ أَنْزَلْنَا هَٰذَا الْقُرْآنَ عَلَىٰ جَبَلٍ لَرَأَيْتَهُ خَاشِعًا مُتَصَدِّعًا مِنْ خَشْيَةِ اللَّهِ ۚ وَتِلْكَ الْأَمْثَالُ نَضْرِبُهَا لِلنَّاسِ لَعَلَّهُمْ يَتَفَكَّرُونَ

٢٢ هُوَ اللَّهُ الَّذِي لَا إِلَٰهَ إِلَّا هُوَ ۖ عَالِمُ الْغَيْبِ وَالشَّهَادَةِ ۖ هُوَ الرَّحْمَٰنُ الرَّحِيمُ

٢٣   هُوَ اللَّهُ الَّذِي لَا إِلَٰهَ إِلَّا هُوَ الْمَلِكُ الْقُدُّوسُ السَّلَامُ الْمُؤْمِنُ الْمُهَيْمِنُ الْعَزِيزُ الْجَبَّارُ الْمُتَكَبِّرُ ۚ سُبْحَانَ اللَّهِ عَمَّا يُشْرِكُونَ

٢٤   هُوَ اللَّهُ الْخَالِقُ الْبَارِئُ الْمُصَوِّرُ ۖ لَهُ الْأَسْمَاءُ الْحُسْنَىٰ ۚ يُسَبِّحُ لَهُ مَا فِي السَّمَاوَاتِ وَالْأَرْضِ ۖ وَهُوَ الْعَزِيزُ الْحَكِيمُ

Surah 59 Transliteration

Bismillahir Rahmanir Rahim

1. Sabbaha lillaahi maa fissamaawaati wa maa fil ardi wa Huwal 'Azeezul Hakeem

2. Huwal lazee akhrajal lazeena kafaroo min ahlil kitaabi min diyaarihim li awwalil Hashr; maa zanantum any yakhrujoo wa zannoo annahum maa ni'atuhum husoonuhum minal laahi faataahumul laahu min haythu lam yahtasiboo wa qazafa fee quloobihimur ru'ba yukhriboona bu yootahum bi aydeehim wa aydil mu'mineena fa'tabiroo yaa ulil absaar

3. Wa law laa an katabal laahu 'alayhimul jalaa ala'azzabahum fid dunyaa wa lahum fil Aakhirati 'azaabun Naar

4. Zaalika bi annahum shaaqqul laaha wa Rasoolahoo wa many yushaaqqil laaha fa innal laaha shadeedul'iqaab

5. Maa qata'tum mil leenatin aw tarak tumoohaa qaa'imatan'alaa usoolihaa fabi iznil laahi wa liyukhziyal faasiqeen

6. Wa maa afaa'allaahu 'alaa Rasoolihee minhum famaa aw jaftum 'alayhi min khailiinw wa laa rikaabinw wa laakinnal laaha yusallitu Rusulahoo 'alaa maiy yashaa'; wallaahu 'alaa kulli shai'in Qadeer

7. Maa afaa'allaahu 'alaa Rasoolihee min ahlil quraa falillahi wa lir Rasooli wa lizil qurbaa wal yataamaa walmasaakeeni wa banis sabeeli kaylaa yakoona doolatam baynal aghniyaa'i minkum; wa maa aataakumur Rasoolu fakhuzoohu wa maa nahaakum 'anhu fantahoo; wattaqullaah. Innallaaha shadeedul-'iqaab

8. Lilfuqaraa'il Muhaaji reenal lazeena ukhrijoo min diyaarihim wa amwaalihim yabtaghoona fadlam minallaahi wa ridwaanan wa yansuroonal laaha wa Rasoolah; ulaa-ika humus sawdiqoon

9. Wallazeena tabawwa 'ud-daara wal eemaana min qablihim yuhibboona man haajara ilayhim wa laa yajidoona fee sudoorihim haajatam mimmaa ootoo wa

yu'thiroona 'alaa anfusihim wa law kaana bihim khasaasah; wa maiy yooqa shuhha nafsihee fa ulaa-ika humul muflihoon

10.   Wallazeena jaa'oo min ba'dihim yaqooloona Rabbanagh fir lanaa wa li ikhwaani nal lazeena sabqoonaa bil eemaani wa laa taj'al fee quloobinaa ghillalil lazeena aamanoo rabbannaa innaka Ra'oofur Raheem

11.   Alam tara ilal lazeena naafaqoo yaqooloona li ikhwaanihimul lazeena kafaroo min ahlil kitaabi la'in ukhrijtum lanakhrujanna ma'akum wa laa nutee'u feekum ahadan abadan wa-in qootiltum lanansuran nakum wallaahu yashhadu innahum lakaaziboon

12.   La'in ukhrijoo laa yakhrujoona ma'ahum wa la'in qootiloo laa yansuroonahum wa la'in nasaroohum la yuwallunnal adbaara thumma laa yunsaroon

13.   La antum ashaddu rahbatan fee sudoorihim minallaah; zaalika bi annahum qawmul laa yafqahoon

14.   Laa yuqaatiloonakum jamee'an illaa fee quram muhas sanatin aw min waraa'i judur; baasuhum baynahum shadeed; tah sabuhum jamee'an wa

47

quloobuhum shatta; zaalika bi annahum qawmul laa ya'qiloon

15. Kamathalil lazeena min qablihim qareeban zaaqoo wabaala amrihim wa lahum 'azaabun aleem

16. Kamathalish shyitaani izqaala lil insaanik fur fa lammaa kafara qaala innee baree'um minka innee akhaafullaaha rabbal 'aalameen

17. Fakaana 'aaqibata humaa anna humaa fin naari khaalidayni feehaa; wa zaalika jazaa'uz zaalimeen

18. Yaa ayyuhal lazeena aamanu taqul-laaha; waltanzur nafsum maa qaddamat lighadiw wattaquallaah; innal laaha khabeerum bimaa ta'maloon

19. Wa laa takoonoo kallazeena nasul laaha fa ansaahum anfusahum; ulaa-ika humul faasiqoon

20. Laa yastawee as-haabun naari wa ashaabul jannah; as haabul jannati humul faa-izoon

21. Law anzalnaa haazal quraana 'alaa jabilil lara aytahoo khaashi'am muta saddi'am min khashiyatil laah; wa tilkal amsaalu nadribuhaa linnaasi la'allahum yatafakkaroon

22.   Huwal-laahul-lazee laa Ilaaha illaa Huwa 'Aalimul Ghaybi wash-shahaada; Huwar Rahmaanur-Raheem

23.   Huwal-laahul-lazee laa ilaaha illaa Huwal Malikul Quddoosus Salaamul Mu-minul Muhayminul 'Azeezul Jabbaarul Mutakabbir; Soob haanal laahi 'Ammaa yushrikoon

24.   Huwal Laahul Khaaliqul Baari 'ul Musawwir; lahul Asmaa'ul Husnaa; yusabbihu lahoo maa fis samaawaati wal ardi wa Huwal 'Azeezul Hakeem

She Who is Interviewed

60 Al Mumtahinah
Middle to Late Medinan Period

☞ Introduction

This chapter was revealed just after the Meccans had broken the terms of the Treaty of Hudaybiyyah, and just before the Prophet led an army to Mecca to force its surrender. It reminds the community about the need for group loyalty and warns them of the cruelty they would suffer if the pagans ever had power over them. It also offers the idea that enemies may one day be friends, so believers must not go to extremes in their battles against their opponents.

In the Name of Allah,
the Compassionate, the Merciful

Background Info... v. 1

Some time after the Battle of Badr but before the Conquest of Mecca, a pagan woman from Mecca named Sarah, who had been an entertainer, entered Medina and asked the Prophet to show her mercy due to her being a member of his tribe. Even though she did not convert to Islam, the Prophet allowed her to stay in Medina.

Later on, after the Meccans violated the terms of the treaty of Hudaybiyyah, and while the Prophet was making preparations to march on the city, a concerned Immigrant Muslim named Hatib ibn Abi Balta'a was afraid for his relatives in Mecca, for they were not members of the tribe of Quraysh but were from another smaller tribe.

He thought that he should warn them so Hatib hired Sarah to carry a secret letter to Mecca, warning the Quraysh of the Prophet's arrival, in the hopes of getting them to look after his non-Qurayshi relatives.

The Prophet learned of this scheme and sent some of his followers to find Sarah. They found her and took the letter. The Prophet forgave Hatib because he had served in the Battle of Badr. *(Asbab ul-Nuzul)*

All you who believe! Don't take our mutual enemies for best friends. You're friendly towards them, even though they're denying the truth that's come to you.

They drove you and the Messenger (out of Mecca) only because you believed in your Lord Allah.

If you've really committed yourselves to struggle in My cause and to seek My pleasure, then don't secretly build bonds of friendship with them, for I know what you conceal and what you reveal.

Whoever among you disobeys Me, then he has strayed far from the way. [1]

Why Support Those Who Would Ruin You?

> **Background Info... v. 2-3**
>
> This passage is a reminder to Hatib and others like him, who thought he might tell Allah on Judgment Day that he did what he did for the sake of his relatives and children. He didn't realize that the Meccans were not true to their word and that if they felt they could get away with it or get some gain from it, they would kill his relatives, as well. (*Asbab ul-Nuzul*)

If they were ever to gain an advantage over you, they would treat you like **enemies** - harming you with their hands and tongues in their relentless efforts to destroy your faith. [2]

(And if you were then to reject your faith), neither your relatives nor your children would be of any use to you on the Day of Assembly when He will judge between you, and Allah is watching everything you do. [3]

Be Firm and be Open at the Same Time

There's an excellent example for you that can be found in (the life of) Ibraheem and his (followers) when he declared to his people, "*We're not going to have anything more to do with you or the idols you worship in place of Allah. We reject your (traditions)!*

"*Never again shall there be any friendship or family ties between us and you until you believe in the One God.*"

However, (it wasn't an appropriate act) when Ibraheem said to his father, "*I'm going to ask forgiveness for you, but it's not in my power to obtain anything from Allah on your behalf.*"

(Ibraheem later realized his error and prayed):

"*Our Lord, we place our trust in You, and we **repent** to You, for our final end is with You.* [4]

"*Our Lord, don't make us a test for the faithless; rather, forgive us (our shortcomings), for You are the Powerful and the Wise.*" [5]

Thus, in their example there is a fine pattern for you to emulate – for anyone who hopes in Allah and the Last Day.

However, if anyone turns away, (know that) Allah is the Self-sufficient and is Worthy of All Praise. [6]

It just may be that Allah will create love between you and your enemies, for Allah is capable enough (to bring that about), and Allah is forgiving and merciful. [7]

Allah doesn't forbid you from being kind and fair to those who don't fight you because of your beliefs or drive you from your homes, for Allah loves the **tolerant**. [8]

Allah only forbids you from having relationships with those who fought you for your faith and drove you from your homes or aided in your exile. Whoever befriends one of these, then they're wrongdoers. [9]

Background Info... v. 10-12

The Treaty of Hudaybiyyah said (very unfairly) that the Muslims had to return back to Mecca any man from there who joined Islam afterwards, (if the Meccans demanded it).

This was a hard test for the Muslims, and even at the very moment of signing the treaty, the Prophet was forced to surrender a Meccan convert named Abu Jundal, who had escaped his tormentors and begged the Prophet's protection.

Abu Jundal was taken into custody by the Meccans, but he escaped again and this time fled to the hills. In time, he came to lead a growing band of other Meccan converts, living as bandits, attacking Meccan caravans of their own accord.

Eventually, the Meccans dropped their insistence on the return of their own family members, and these 'warriors of the hills' were allowed to enter Medina.

Women who wanted to convert, however, left straight for the sanctuary of Medina. One such woman named Umm Kulthum bint 'Uqbah fled to join the Muslims (along with her two brothers).

When her pagan relatives came after her and demanded the Prophet return all three of them, the Prophet pointed out that the treaty said, "...any Meccan *man*..."

Then this passage was revealed, and the Prophet said that no woman who wanted to join the Muslims would be returned, though he returned the two brothers regretfully.
(*Asbab ul-Nuzul, Ma'ariful Qur'an*)

All you who believe! When believing women come to you as refugees (from enemy territory), interview them to establish the truth of their convictions, although Allah knows best their true level of faith.

If you determine that they're sincere **believers**, then don't send them back to the faithless.

(Believing women) are no longer legitimate for them (as wives,) even as (idol-worshippers) are no longer legitimate (as husbands for women of faith).

Pay back (the idol-worshippers) for what they spent (on their marriage gifts to the women who have now deserted them). Then there will be no blame if you (believing men seek to) marry (such women) after offering them a marriage gift.

There is no Legal Marriage with an Idol-Worshipper

As for any women (who are idol-worshippers, they're no longer your responsibility), so don't play host to them.

Ask for the dowry you gave to them from (the idol-worshippers), even as they may seek what they spent (on the women joining you).

This is the law of Allah and His judgment between you. Allah is full of knowledge and wisdom. [10]

Compensating the Enemy for Women who Join You

If any of your wives abandon you to be among the faithless, and (one of their women chooses to be among you) in exchange, (even though this cancels out the obligation of both communities), still compensate (the deserted husband) with the value of his (marriage gift) that he had spent. Be mindful of Allah, the One in Whom you've believed. [11]

O Prophet, when believing women come to you and swear this promise of loyalty, that they:

- Won't serve anything other than Allah.
- That they won't steal.
- That they won't commit adultery.
- That they won't kill their (newborn) children.
- That they won't produce any lie that they've invented between their hands or feet.
- Or disobey you in any good act.

53

Then accept their allegiance and pray to Allah for their forgiveness, for Allah is forgiving and merciful. [12]

Don't Betray Your Own Cause

Background Info... v. 13

Some very poor Muslims were selling information on events within the Muslim community to some local Jews who paid them for the intelligence-gathering. This verse was revealed, forbidding contact with those Jews who were encouraging this trade. *(Asbab ul-Nuzul)*

All you who believe! Don't take (for friends) people upon whom is the wrath of Allah. They've already lost all hope of the next life, even as the faithless have lost all hope of ever seeing their buried (ancestors) again. [13]

☁️ Think About It

1. We can be friends with a non-Muslim, as long as they are not trying to insult or destroy our way of life or faith in Allah. Why is it bad to be friends someone like that?

2. What would an enemy of Allah do to us, if they ever got power over us?

3. Why do you think the Qur'an is saying that Prophet Ibraheem should not ask Allah to forgive his father, who worshipped idols and tried to destroy the beliefs of his own son?

4. According to verses 7-8, why should we still always try to be friendly and fair to non-Muslims who are nice to us?

5. When women went to the Prophet to accept Islam, he asked them to agree to follow six rules in verse 12. Which one do you think is most important and why?

Fill in the Words on the lines below.
Look at the **BOLD** words in the main text to see where they go

Words to Use

Repent   Believers   Enemies   Tolerant

---

1. If you determine that they're sincere _____, then don't send them back to the faithless.

2. *"Our Lord, we place our trust in You, and we _____ to You, for our final end is with You.*

3. If they were ever to gain an advantage over you, they would treat you like _____.

4. Allah doesn't forbid you from being kind and fair to those who don't fight you because of your beliefs or drive you from your homes, for Allah loves the _____.

Complete the Crossword Puzzle Below

(Words can be in any direction, even backwards!)

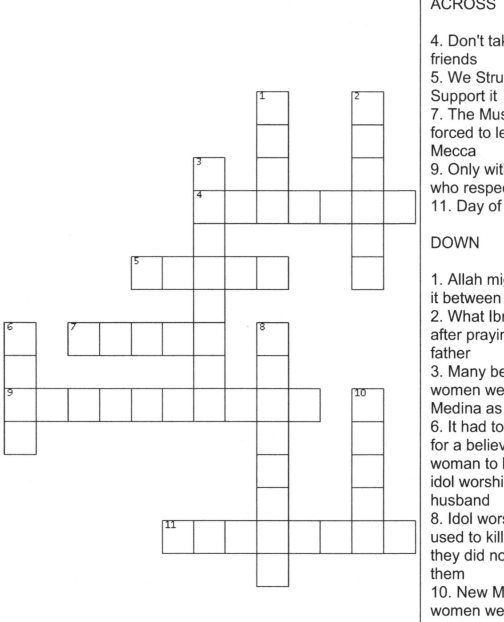

ACROSS

4. Don't take them for friends
5. We Struggle to Support it
7. The Muslims were forced to leave Mecca
9. Only with people who respect us
11. Day of

DOWN

1. Allah might create it between you
2. What Ibrahim did after praying for his father
3. Many believing women went to Medina as
6. It had to be repaid for a believing woman to leave her idol worshipping husband
8. Idol worshippers used to kill them if they did not want them
10. New Muslim women were asked not to do this

Arabic Text

بِسْمِ اللهِ الرَّحْمٰنِ الرَّحِيمِ

١ يَا أَيُّهَا الَّذِينَ آمَنُوا لَا تَتَّخِذُوا عَدُوِّي وَعَدُوَّكُمْ أَوْلِيَاءَ تُلْقُونَ إِلَيْهِمْ بِالْمَوَدَّةِ وَقَدْ كَفَرُوا بِمَا جَاءَكُمْ مِنَ الْحَقِّ يُخْرِجُونَ الرَّسُولَ وَإِيَّاكُمْ أَنْ تُؤْمِنُوا بِاللهِ رَبِّكُمْ إِنْ كُنْتُمْ خَرَجْتُمْ جِهَادًا فِي سَبِيلِي وَابْتِغَاءَ مَرْضَاتِي تُسِرُّونَ إِلَيْهِمْ بِالْمَوَدَّةِ وَأَنَا أَعْلَمُ بِمَا أَخْفَيْتُمْ وَمَا أَعْلَنْتُمْ وَمَنْ يَفْعَلْهُ مِنْكُمْ فَقَدْ ضَلَّ سَوَاءَ السَّبِيلِ

٢ إِنْ يَثْقَفُوكُمْ يَكُونُوا لَكُمْ أَعْدَاءً وَيَبْسُطُوا إِلَيْكُمْ أَيْدِيَهُمْ وَأَلْسِنَتَهُمْ بِالسُّوءِ وَوَدُّوا لَوْ تَكْفُرُونَ

٣ لَنْ تَنْفَعَكُمْ أَرْحَامُكُمْ وَلَا أَوْلَادُكُمْ يَوْمَ الْقِيَامَةِ يَفْصِلُ بَيْنَكُمْ وَاللهُ بِمَا تَعْمَلُونَ بَصِيرٌ

٤ قَدْ كَانَتْ لَكُمْ أُسْوَةٌ حَسَنَةٌ فِي إِبْرَاهِيمَ وَالَّذِينَ مَعَهُ إِذْ قَالُوا لِقَوْمِهِمْ إِنَّا بُرَآءُ مِنْكُمْ وَمِمَّا تَعْبُدُونَ مِنْ دُونِ اللهِ كَفَرْنَا بِكُمْ وَبَدَا بَيْنَنَا وَبَيْنَكُمُ الْعَدَاوَةُ وَالْبَغْضَاءُ أَبَدًا حَتَّى تُؤْمِنُوا بِاللهِ وَحْدَهُ إِلَّا قَوْلَ إِبْرَاهِيمَ لِأَبِيهِ لَأَسْتَغْفِرَنَّ لَكَ وَمَا أَمْلِكُ لَكَ مِنَ اللهِ مِنْ شَيْءٍ رَبَّنَا عَلَيْكَ تَوَكَّلْنَا وَإِلَيْكَ أَنَبْنَا وَإِلَيْكَ الْمَصِيرُ

٥ رَبَّنَا لَا تَجْعَلْنَا فِتْنَةً لِلَّذِينَ كَفَرُوا وَاغْفِرْ لَنَا رَبَّنَا إِنَّكَ أَنْتَ الْعَزِيزُ الْحَكِيمُ

٦ لَقَدْ كَانَ لَكُمْ فِيهِمْ أُسْوَةٌ حَسَنَةٌ لِمَنْ كَانَ يَرْجُو اللَّهَ وَالْيَوْمَ الْآخِرَ وَمَن يَتَوَلَّ فَإِنَّ اللَّهَ هُوَ الْغَنِيُّ الْحَمِيدُ

٧ عَسَى اللَّهُ أَن يَجْعَلَ بَيْنَكُمْ وَبَيْنَ الَّذِينَ عَادَيْتُم مِّنْهُم مَّوَدَّةً ۚ وَاللَّهُ قَدِيرٌ ۚ وَاللَّهُ غَفُورٌ رَّحِيمٌ

٨ لَا يَنْهَاكُمُ اللَّهُ عَنِ الَّذِينَ لَمْ يُقَاتِلُوكُمْ فِي الدِّينِ وَلَمْ يُخْرِجُوكُم مِّن دِيَارِكُمْ أَن تَبَرُّوهُمْ وَتُقْسِطُوا إِلَيْهِمْ ۚ إِنَّ اللَّهَ يُحِبُّ الْمُقْسِطِينَ

٩ إِنَّمَا يَنْهَاكُمُ اللَّهُ عَنِ الَّذِينَ قَاتَلُوكُمْ فِي الدِّينِ وَأَخْرَجُوكُم مِّن دِيَارِكُمْ وَظَاهَرُوا عَلَىٰ إِخْرَاجِكُمْ أَن تَوَلَّوْهُمْ ۚ وَمَن يَتَوَلَّهُمْ فَأُولَٰئِكَ هُمُ الظَّالِمُونَ

١٠ يَا أَيُّهَا الَّذِينَ آمَنُوا إِذَا جَاءَكُمُ الْمُؤْمِنَاتُ مُهَاجِرَاتٍ فَامْتَحِنُوهُنَّ ۖ اللَّهُ أَعْلَمُ بِإِيمَانِهِنَّ ۖ فَإِنْ عَلِمْتُمُوهُنَّ مُؤْمِنَاتٍ فَلَا تَرْجِعُوهُنَّ إِلَى الْكُفَّارِ ۖ لَا هُنَّ حِلٌّ لَّهُمْ وَلَا هُمْ يَحِلُّونَ لَهُنَّ ۖ وَآتُوهُم مَّا أَنفَقُوا ۚ وَلَا جُنَاحَ عَلَيْكُمْ أَن تَنكِحُوهُنَّ إِذَا آتَيْتُمُوهُنَّ أُجُورَهُنَّ ۚ وَلَا تُمْسِكُوا بِعِصَمِ الْكَوَافِرِ وَاسْأَلُوا مَا أَنفَقْتُمْ وَلْيَسْأَلُوا مَا أَنفَقُوا ۚ ذَٰلِكُمْ حُكْمُ اللَّهِ ۖ يَحْكُمُ بَيْنَكُمْ ۚ وَاللَّهُ عَلِيمٌ حَكِيمٌ

١١ وَإِن فَاتَكُمْ شَيْءٌ مِّنْ أَزْوَاجِكُمْ إِلَى الْكُفَّارِ فَعَاقَبْتُمْ فَآتُوا الَّذِينَ ذَهَبَتْ أَزْوَاجُهُم مِّثْلَ مَا أَنفَقُوا ۚ وَاتَّقُوا اللَّهَ الَّذِي أَنتُم بِهِ مُؤْمِنُونَ

١٢ يَا أَيُّهَا النَّبِيُّ إِذَا جَاءَكَ الْمُؤْمِنَاتُ يُبَايِعْنَكَ عَلَىٰ أَنْ لَا يُشْرِكْنَ بِاللَّهِ شَيْئًا وَلَا يَسْرِقْنَ وَلَا يَزْنِينَ وَلَا يَقْتُلْنَ أَوْلَادَهُنَّ وَلَا يَأْتِينَ بِبُهْتَانٍ يَفْتَرِينَهُ بَيْنَ أَيْدِيهِنَّ وَأَرْجُلِهِنَّ وَلَا يَعْصِينَكَ فِي مَعْرُوفٍ ۙ فَبَايِعْهُنَّ وَاسْتَغْفِرْ لَهُنَّ اللَّهَ ۖ إِنَّ اللَّهَ غَفُورٌ رَحِيمٌ

١٣ يَا أَيُّهَا الَّذِينَ آمَنُوا لَا تَتَوَلَّوْا قَوْمًا غَضِبَ اللَّهُ عَلَيْهِمْ قَدْ يَئِسُوا مِنَ الْآخِرَةِ كَمَا يَئِسَ الْكُفَّارُ مِنْ أَصْحَابِ الْقُبُورِ

Surah 60 Transliteration

Bismillahir Rahmanir Rahim

1. Yaa ayyuhal lazeena aamanoo laa tattakhizoo 'aduwwee wa 'aduwaakum awliyaa'a tulqoona ilayhim bil mawaddati wa qad kafaroo bima jaa'akum minal haqq, yukh rijoonar Rasoola wa iyyaakum an tu'minoo bil laahi rabbikum in kuntum kharajtum jihaadan fee sabeelee wabtighaa'a mardaatee; tusirroona ilayhim bilma waddati wa ana a'alamu bimaa akhfaytum wa maa a'lantum; wa maiy yaf'alhu minkum faqad dalla sawaa'as sabeel

2. Iy-yath qafookum yakoonoo lakum a'daa'an wa yabsutoo ilaykum aydiyahum wa alsinatahum bissoo'l wa waddoo law takfuroon

3. Lan tanfa'akum arhaamukum wa laa awlaadukum; yawmal qiyaamati yafsilu baynakum; wallaahu bimaa ta'maloon baseer

4. Qad kaanat lakum uswatun hasanatun fee Ibraaheema wallazeena ma'ahoo iz qaaloo liqawmihim innaa bura

60

'aa'u minkum wa mimmaa ta'budoona min doonil laahi kafarnaa bikum wa badaa baynanaa wa baynakumul 'adaawatu wal baghdaa'u abadan hattaa tu'minoo billaahi wahdahoo illaa qawla Ibraheema li abeehi la astaghfiranna laka wa maa amliku laka minallaahi min shay; rabbanaa 'alayka tawakkalnaa wa ilayka anabnaa wa ilaykal maseer

5. Rabbana laa taj'alnaa fitnatal lillazeena kafaroo waghfir lanaa rabbanaa innaka antal azeezul hakeem

6. Laqad kaana lakum feehim uswa tun hasanatul liman kaana yarjul laaha wal yawmal aakhir; wa maiy yatawalla fa innal laaha huwal ghaniyyul hameed

7. Asallaahu aiy yaj'ala baynakum wa baynal lazeena 'aadaytum minhum mawaddah; wallahu qadeer; wallahu ghafoorur raheem

8. Laa yanhaakumullaahu 'anil lazeena lam yuqaatilookum fid deeni wa lam yukhrijookum min diyaarikum an tabar roohum wa tuqsitoo ilayhim; innallaaha yuhibbul muqsiteen

9. Innamaa yanhaakumullaahu 'anil lazeena qaatalookum fid deeni wa akhrajookum min diyaarikum wa zaaharoo

'alaa ikhraajikum an tawallawhum; wa maiy yatawallahum fa ulaa-ika humuz zaalimoon

10.   Yaa ayyuhal lazeena aamanoo izaa jaa'akumul mu'minaatu muhaajiraatin fam tahinoo hunn; Allaahu a'lamu bi eemaani hinn; fa in 'alimtumoo hunna mu'minaatin falaa tarji'oo hunna ilal kuffaar; laa hunna hillul lahum wa laa hum yahilloona lahunna wa aatoohum maa anfaqoo wa laa junaaha 'alaykum an tankihoohunna izaa aataityu moohunna ujoorahunn; wa laa tumsikoo bi 'isamil kawaafir; was -aloo maa anfaqtum walyas -aloo maa anfaqoo; zaalikum hukmul laahi yahkumu baynakum; wallaahu 'aleemun hakeem

11.   Wa in faatakum shay-un min azwaajikum ilal kuffaari fa 'aaqabtum fa aatul lazeena zahabat azwaajuhum misla maa anfaqoo; wattaq ullaah allazee antum bihee mu'minoon

12.   Yaa ayyuhan nabbiyyu izaa jaa'akal mu'minaatu yubaayigh'naka 'alaa allaa yushrikna billaahi shaiy-an wa laa yasriqna wa laa yazneena wa laa yaqtulna awlaadahunna wa laa ya'teena bibuh taaniy yaftaree nahoo bayna aydeehinna wa arjulihinna wa laa

ya'seenaka fee ma'roofin fa baayigh' hunna wastaghfir

lahunnallah; innallaaha ghafoorur raheem

13.   Yaa ayyuhal lazeena amanoo laa tatawallaw

qawman ghadiballaahu 'alayhim qad ya'isoo minal

aakhirati kamaa ya'isal kuffaaru min as haabil quboor

The Formations

61 As-Saff
Early Medinan Period

☞ Introduction

This chapter opens with a reference to the failure of some of Muhammad's (p) followers to obey orders during the Battle of Uhud. Of fifty archers he had placed on a hill to guard his rear position, nearly all of them abandoned their posts to collect the goods the pagans of Mecca dropped when they were fleeing the battlefield in confusion. (The few who had remained at their post were overwhelmed by the advancing Meccan cavalry.)

This violation of orders allowed the Meccan cavalry to counterattack and turn the tide against the Muslims, who were nearly crushed in defeat. Only a spirited defense saved the Muslims from being annihilated in the fearsome melee that followed.

In the Name of Allah,
the Compassionate, the Merciful

All things within the heavens and the earth reflect the glory of Allah, for He is the Powerful and the Wise.

All you who (claim) to believe! Why do you say what you don't do? It's terrible in Allah's sight to say what you don't do. [1-3]

Allah loves those who struggle in His cause in **straight** lines, as if they were a brick wall, (rather than those who disobey orders). [4]

Remember when Musa said to his people, "*My people! Why are you causing me so much grief when you know that I'm the Messenger of Allah sent to you?*"

When they wavered (from their duty), Allah allowed their hearts to waver even further, for Allah doesn't guide rebellious people. [5]

Remember that 'Esa, the son of Maryam, (also faced a similar challenge) when he announced, "*Children of Israel! I'm the Messenger of Allah sent to you.*

"I confirm the truth of the Torah that came before me, and I bring you the good news of a messenger who will come after me, whose name will mean 'praise'."

However, when (the foretold prophet) came to them with clear evidence (of the truth), they scoffed, "*This (message he brings) is obviously some kind of **magic!***" [6]

Who's more corrupt than the one who invents such lies against Allah, especially when he's only being called to surrender his will (to Allah)? Allah doesn't guide corrupt people. [7]

They want to dim the light of Allah with their mouths (by attacking His revelations), though Allah will spread His light fully, no matter how much the faithless may hate it. [8]

He's the One Who sent His Messenger with guidance and the way of truth, so that he could proclaim it over all (other) ways of life, no matter how much the idol-worshippers may hate it. [9]

The Cause of Allah

All you who believe! Shall I lead you to a bargain that will save you from a painful punishment? [10]

Just believe in Allah and His Messenger; then struggle in the cause of Allah with your wealth and your lives. That's the best (deal) for you if you only knew! [11]

He'll forgive you your sins and admit you to gardens beneath which rivers flow and to stunning mansions in beautiful gardens of eternity. That's the greatest success! [12]

He'll also grant you something else you ardently desire: help from Allah and a swift **victory**. So then announce the good news to all who believe! [13]

All you who believe! Be disciples in the cause of Allah, even as 'Esa, the son of Maryam, called for disciples, saying, "*Who will **help** me (to call the people to) Allah?*"

Then the disciples (joined him and) declared, "*We shall help you (call the people to) Allah.*"

It just so happened that some of the Children of Israel believed, while others rejected faith, but We reinforced the believers against their enemies, and they ultimately prevailed. [14]

☁ Think About It

1. Why is it hard to be successful if some people don't follow directions?

2. Look at verse 5. What is Allah trying to tell the Muslims about how they are treating Prophet Muhammad?

3. Look at verse 6. How is this similar to the way the idol worshippers of Mecca were treating the Prophet?

4. What is the bargain Allah is offering us, and how do we get it?

5. In verse 14, every Muslim is asked to do what? How do we implement that in our lives?

Fill in the Words on the lines below.
Look at the **BOLD** words in the main text to see where they go

Words to Use

Magic   Victory   Help   Straight

---

1. Allah loves those who struggle in His cause in _____ lines, as if they were a brick wall

2. *"This (message he brings) is obviously some kind of _____!"*

3. He'll also grant you something else you ardently desire: help from Allah and a swift _____.

4. *"We shall _____ you (call the people to) Allah."*

Complete the Crossword Puzzle Below

(Words can be in any direction, even backwards!)

ACROSS

1. Why do you do this and then not do?
3. Of Allah cannot be dimmed
5. Unbelievers call Allah's message some kind of...
7. Allah will spread it fully
8. The Mother of 'Esa
10. English name for 'Esa
11. Of Israel
12. Allah is offering this to us
13. Allah will not guide these people

DOWN

1. Victory
2. What people give to their Prophets
4. The Book of Musa
6. Have no power
9. Of Allah

Arabic Text

بسم الله الرحمن الرحيم

١ سَبَّحَ لِلَّهِ مَا فِي السَّمَاوَاتِ وَمَا فِي الْأَرْضِ ۖ وَهُوَ الْعَزِيزُ الْحَكِيمُ

٢ يَا أَيُّهَا الَّذِينَ آمَنُوا لِمَ تَقُولُونَ مَا لَا تَفْعَلُونَ

٣ كَبُرَ مَقْتًا عِنْدَ اللَّهِ أَنْ تَقُولُوا مَا لَا تَفْعَلُونَ

٤ إِنَّ اللَّهَ يُحِبُّ الَّذِينَ يُقَاتِلُونَ فِي سَبِيلِهِ صَفًّا كَأَنَّهُمْ بُنْيَانٌ مَرْصُوصٌ

٥ وَإِذْ قَالَ مُوسَىٰ لِقَوْمِهِ يَا قَوْمِ لِمَ تُؤْذُونَنِي وَقَدْ تَعْلَمُونَ أَنِّي رَسُولُ اللَّهِ إِلَيْكُمْ ۖ فَلَمَّا زَاغُوا أَزَاغَ اللَّهُ قُلُوبَهُمْ ۚ وَاللَّهُ لَا يَهْدِي الْقَوْمَ الْفَاسِقِينَ

٦ وَإِذْ قَالَ عِيسَى ابْنُ مَرْيَمَ يَا بَنِي إِسْرَائِيلَ إِنِّي رَسُولُ اللَّهِ إِلَيْكُمْ مُصَدِّقًا لِمَا بَيْنَ يَدَيَّ مِنَ التَّوْرَاةِ وَمُبَشِّرًا بِرَسُولٍ يَأْتِي مِنْ بَعْدِي اسْمُهُ أَحْمَدُ ۖ فَلَمَّا جَاءَهُمْ بِالْبَيِّنَاتِ قَالُوا هَٰذَا سِحْرٌ مُبِينٌ

٧ وَمَنْ أَظْلَمُ مِمَّنِ افْتَرَىٰ عَلَى اللَّهِ الْكَذِبَ وَهُوَ يُدْعَىٰ إِلَى الْإِسْلَامِ وَاللَّهُ لَا يَهْدِي الْقَوْمَ الظَّالِمِينَ

٨ يُرِيدُونَ لِيُطْفِئُوا نُورَ اللَّهِ بِأَفْوَاهِهِمْ وَاللَّهُ مُتِمُّ نُورِهِ وَلَوْ كَرِهَ الْكَافِرُونَ

٩ هُوَ الَّذِي أَرْسَلَ رَسُولَهُ بِالْهُدَىٰ وَدِينِ الْحَقِّ لِيُظْهِرَهُ عَلَى الدِّينِ كُلِّهِ وَلَوْ كَرِهَ الْمُشْرِكُونَ

١٠ يَا أَيُّهَا الَّذِينَ آمَنُوا هَلْ أَدُلُّكُمْ عَلَىٰ تِجَارَةٍ تُنْجِيكُمْ مِنْ عَذَابٍ أَلِيمٍ

١١ تُؤْمِنُونَ بِاللَّهِ وَرَسُولِهِ وَتُجَاهِدُونَ فِي سَبِيلِ اللَّهِ بِأَمْوَالِكُمْ وَأَنْفُسِكُمْ ۚ ذَٰلِكُمْ خَيْرٌ لَكُمْ إِنْ كُنْتُمْ تَعْلَمُونَ

١٢ يَغْفِرْ لَكُمْ ذُنُوبَكُمْ وَيُدْخِلْكُمْ جَنَّاتٍ تَجْرِي مِنْ تَحْتِهَا الْأَنْهَارُ وَمَسَاكِنَ طَيِّبَةً فِي جَنَّاتِ عَدْنٍ ۚ ذَٰلِكَ الْفَوْزُ الْعَظِيمُ

١٣ وَأُخْرَىٰ تُحِبُّونَهَا ۖ نَصْرٌ مِنَ اللَّهِ وَفَتْحٌ قَرِيبٌ ۗ وَبَشِّرِ الْمُؤْمِنِينَ

١٤ يَا أَيُّهَا الَّذِينَ آمَنُوا كُونُوا أَنْصَارَ اللَّهِ كَمَا قَالَ عِيسَى ابْنُ مَرْيَمَ لِلْحَوَارِيِّينَ مَنْ أَنْصَارِي إِلَى اللَّهِ ۖ قَالَ الْحَوَارِيُّونَ نَحْنُ أَنْصَارُ اللَّهِ فَآمَنَتْ طَائِفَةٌ مِنْ بَنِي إِسْرَائِيلَ وَكَفَرَتْ طَائِفَةٌ ۖ فَأَيَّدْنَا الَّذِينَ آمَنُوا عَلَىٰ عَدُوِّهِمْ فَأَصْبَحُوا ظَاهِرِينَ

Surah 61 Transliteration

Bismillahir Rahmanir Rahim

1. Sabbaha lillaahi maa fisamaawaati wa maa fil ardi wa huwal 'Azeezul Hakeem

2. Yaa ayyuhal lazeena aamanoo lima taqooloona maa laa taf'aloon

3. Kabura maqtan 'indallaahi an taqooloo maa laa taf'aloon

4. Innallaaha yuhibbul lazeena yuqaatiloona fee sabeelihee saffan ka annahum bunyaanum marsoos

5. Wa iz qawla Moosa liqawmihee yaa qawmi lima tu'zoonanee wa qat ta'lamoona annee Rasoolul laahi ilaykum falammaa zaaghoo azaaghal laahu quloobahum; wallaahu laa yahdil qawmal faasiqeen

6. Wa iz qawla 'Eesab-nu-Maryama yaa Banee Israa'eela innee Rasoolullaahi ilaykum musaddiqal limaa bayna yadayya minat Tawraati wa mubashiram bi Rasoolin yaatee mim ba'dis muhoo Ahmad; falammaa jaa-ahum bil baiyinaati qaaloo haazaa sihrum mubeen

7. Wa man azlamu mimma nif taraa 'alal laahil kaziba wa huwa yad'aa ilal Islaam; wallaahu laa yahdil qawmaz zaalimeen

8. Yureedoona liyutfi'oo nooral laahi bi afwaahihim wallaahu mutimmu noorihee wa law karihal kaafiroon

9. Huwal lazee arsala Rasoolahoo bil hudaa wa deenil haqqi liyuzhirahoo 'alad deeni kullihee wa law karihal mushrikoon

10.   Yaa ayyuhal lazeena aamanoo hal adullukum 'alaa tijaaratin tunjeekum min 'azaabin aleem

11.   Tu'minoona billaahi wa Rasoolihee wa tujaahidoona fee sabeelillaahi bi amwaalikum wa anfusikum; zaalikum khayrul lakum in kuntum ta'lamoon

12.   Yaghfir lakum zunoobakum wa yud khilkum Jannaatin tajree min tahtihal anhaaru wa masaakina taiyibatan fee Jannaati 'Adn; zaalikal fawzul 'Azeem

13.   Wa ukhraa tuhibboonahaa nasrum minallaahi wa fat hun qareeb; wa bashiril mu-mineen

14.   Yaa ayyuhal lazeena aamanoo koonoo ansaarallaahi kamaa qawla 'Eesab-nu-Maryama lil Hawaariyyeena man ansaaree ilallaah; qawlal Hawaariyyoona nahnu ansaarul

laah. Fa aamanat taa'ifatum mim Bannee Israa'eela wa kafarat taa'ifatun fa ayyadnal lazeena aamanoo 'alaa 'aduwwihim fa asbahoo zaahireen

The Congregation

62 Al Jumu'ah
Mixed Medinan Period

☞ Introduction

The first eight verses of this chapter were sent down in approximately the year 628 after the Muslims forced the capitulation of the northern Jewish settlement of Khaybar. A remnant of the exiled Banu Nadir, who had settled there among their cousins, were responsible for assembling the Grand Alliance of Jews, Meccans and bedouin pagans that had threatened the very existence of the Muslim community during the Great Siege of Medina the prior year. (The Jews of Khaybar were allowed to remain in their settlement, but they had to pay an annual tribute.) The remaining verses were revealed earlier, perhaps in the first year or two after the migration, and cover a real incident that tested the faithfulness of the believers.

Salman al-Farsi, a Persian convert to Islam, was sitting with the Prophet in a gathering when the first eight verses of this chapter were revealed. When the Prophet reached verse three, Salman asked excitedly, "Messenger of Allah! Who are the (people of the other nations who will accept Islam)?" The Prophet remained silent, and Salman asked the same question again. Then the Prophet placed his hand on Salman's shoulder and told the people, "Even if faith were as far away as the highest stars in the sky, still some of these (Persians) would have accepted it." *(Bukhari)*

In the Name of Allah,
the Compassionate, the Merciful

All things within the heavens and on the earth reflect the glory of Allah. He's the King, the Holy, the Powerful and the Wise. [1]

He's the One Who raised a messenger from an unschooled nation - a messenger from among their own kind to recite revealed verses from Him, to reform them, to teach them the scripture and to give them wisdom, for they lived in obvious error before. [2]

(He wants them to spread this message) from themselves to others among them who haven't joined them yet, for He is Powerful and Wise. [3]

That's the **favor** of Allah that He gives to whomever He wills, and Allah is a master at bestowing great favor. [4]

The example of those who were given the Torah before, but who then failed in their duty, is like that of a donkey that carries a load of books, (oblivious to the value of what it bears).

What a disgraceful metaphor for a nation that denied the signs of Allah! Allah doesn't guide corrupted nations. [5]

Tell them, *"All you who follow (the religion of) Judaism! If you claim to be the chosen allies of Allah to the exclusion of all other people, then wish for death (so you can go to Heaven straight away), that is if you're speaking the truth!"* [6]

However, they would never wish for death on account of what their hands have sent ahead of them (for Judgment Day), and Allah knows who the wrongdoers are. [7]

So say to them, *"The death you so ardently avoid will surely overtake you! Then you'll go back to the One Who knows everything that's beyond perception, as well as everything that's in plain sight. Then He'll show you (the real meaning) of everything you did."* [8]

The Importance of Friday Prayer

Background Info... v. 9

The Prophet heard a rushing sound behind him while he was leading the congregation in prayer during one Friday service. After the prayer had ended, he asked about it and was told that some people had rushed in to catch the prayer.

The Prophet asked them, "What's the matter with you?" because the rushing of those people disturbed everyone. The people who came late replied, "We were moving along without delay to prayer," citing this verse.

The Prophet said, "Don't do it like that. When you come for prayer, you should be calm and peaceful. Pray whatever remains of the prayer, and complete what you missed." (*Muslim*)

He also said, "When you come to attend the prayer, don't come in a rush, but rather come to it while walking at ease and gracefully." (*Muslim*)

All you who believe! When the call for Friday prayer is proclaimed, move along without delay to the **remembrance** of Allah, and leave off your business. That's the best thing for you if you only knew. [9]

When the prayer is completed, you may again disperse throughout the land and seek the bounty of Allah. **Remember** Allah a lot so that you may be successful. [10]

Don't be Distracted from Prayer by Worldly Events

> ### Background Info... v. 11
>
> The Prophet was giving a Friday congregational sermon when the sound of drums beating in the street was suddenly heard. (This was how new caravan arrivals were announced in Medina.)
>
> Then someone said that a new caravan from Syria, loaded full of foodstuffs for sale, had arrived in town. There had been a food shortage in the city for some time, so everyone in the congregation (except for twelve men) got up and left the masjid, leaving the stunned Prophet in the middle of his sermon.
>
> This verse was revealed to scold those who forgot their duty to Allah and left a holy act only for the sake of shopping, which they could have done afterwards. (Bukhari, Muslim)

Yet, even still when they see a **chance** to make a deal or have some fun, they run straight towards it, leaving you standing there (alone in the masjid)!

Say to them, *"What you can get from Allah is far better than any entertainment or bargain, for Allah is the best provider of all."* [11]

☁ Think About It

1. What do you think "unschooled nation" means in verse 2?

2. Why are the people who were given the Torah compared to the example of a donkey?

3. What warning is there for Muslims in verse 5, that can also apply to us if we are not careful?

4. When it is time for Friday Prayer, what should a Muslim do?

5. How do some people disrespect the Friday prayer?

Fill in the Words on the lines below.
Look at the **BOLD** words in the main text to see where they go
Words to Use
Favor   Successful   Chance   Remembrance

1. That's the _____ of Allah that He gives to whomever He wills, and Allah is a master at bestowing great favor.

2. When the call for Friday prayer is proclaimed, move along without delay to the _____ of Allah...

3. Remember Allah a lot so that you may be _____.

4. Yet, even still when they see a _____ to make a deal or have some fun, they run straight towards it...

Complete the Crossword Puzzle Below
(Words can be in any direction, even backwards!)

ACROSS

3. People would rather do this than go to Jumu'ah
5. Means not having books in your language
7. Day of
9. Jumu'ah in Arabic
11. Allah wanted to give this to a nation that never had one before
12. Example of people who have a lot of books but don't follow them

DOWN

1. Allah is a master of bestowing
2. Look for it after Jumu'ah is over
4. Of Allah
6. Allah is the best
8. Another word for Example
10. People who do wrong are afraid of it

بسم الله الرحمن الرحيم

١ يُسَبِّحُ لِلَّهِ مَا فِي السَّمَاوَاتِ وَمَا فِي الْأَرْضِ الْمَلِكِ الْقُدُّوسِ الْعَزِيزِ الْحَكِيمِ

٢ هُوَ الَّذِي بَعَثَ فِي الْأُمِّيِّينَ رَسُولًا مِنْهُمْ يَتْلُو عَلَيْهِمْ آيَاتِهِ وَيُزَكِّيهِمْ وَيُعَلِّمُهُمُ الْكِتَابَ وَالْحِكْمَةَ وَإِنْ كَانُوا مِنْ قَبْلُ لَفِي ضَلَالٍ مُبِينٍ

٣ وَآخَرِينَ مِنْهُمْ لَمَّا يَلْحَقُوا بِهِمْ ۚ وَهُوَ الْعَزِيزُ الْحَكِيمُ

٤ ذَٰلِكَ فَضْلُ اللَّهِ يُؤْتِيهِ مَنْ يَشَاءُ ۚ وَاللَّهُ ذُو الْفَضْلِ الْعَظِيمِ

٥ مَثَلُ الَّذِينَ حُمِّلُوا التَّوْرَاةَ ثُمَّ لَمْ يَحْمِلُوهَا كَمَثَلِ الْحِمَارِ يَحْمِلُ أَسْفَارًا ۚ بِئْسَ مَثَلُ الْقَوْمِ الَّذِينَ كَذَّبُوا بِآيَاتِ اللَّهِ ۚ وَاللَّهُ لَا يَهْدِي الْقَوْمَ الظَّالِمِينَ

٦ قُلْ يَا أَيُّهَا الَّذِينَ هَادُوا إِنْ زَعَمْتُمْ أَنَّكُمْ أَوْلِيَاءُ لِلَّهِ مِنْ دُونِ النَّاسِ فَتَمَنَّوُا الْمَوْتَ إِنْ كُنْتُمْ صَادِقِينَ

٧ وَلَا يَتَمَنَّوْنَهُ أَبَدًا بِمَا قَدَّمَتْ أَيْدِيهِمْ ۚ وَاللَّهُ عَلِيمٌ بِالظَّالِمِينَ

٨   قُلْ إِنَّ الْمَوْتَ الَّذِي تَفِرُّونَ مِنْهُ فَإِنَّهُ مُلَاقِيكُمْ ۖ ثُمَّ تُرَدُّونَ إِلَىٰ عَالِمِ الْغَيْبِ وَالشَّهَادَةِ فَيُنَبِّئُكُمْ بِمَا كُنْتُمْ تَعْمَلُونَ

٩   يَا أَيُّهَا الَّذِينَ آمَنُوا إِذَا نُودِيَ لِلصَّلَاةِ مِنْ يَوْمِ الْجُمُعَةِ فَاسْعَوْا إِلَىٰ ذِكْرِ اللَّهِ وَذَرُوا الْبَيْعَ ۚ ذَٰلِكُمْ خَيْرٌ لَكُمْ إِنْ كُنْتُمْ تَعْلَمُونَ

١٠   فَإِذَا قُضِيَتِ الصَّلَاةُ فَانْتَشِرُوا فِي الْأَرْضِ وَابْتَغُوا مِنْ فَضْلِ اللَّهِ وَاذْكُرُوا اللَّهَ كَثِيرًا لَعَلَّكُمْ تُفْلِحُونَ

١١   وَإِذَا رَأَوْا تِجَارَةً أَوْ لَهْوًا انْفَضُّوا إِلَيْهَا وَتَرَكُوكَ قَائِمًا ۚ قُلْ مَا عِنْدَ اللَّهِ خَيْرٌ مِنَ اللَّهْوِ وَمِنَ التِّجَارَةِ ۚ وَاللَّهُ خَيْرُ الرَّازِقِينَ

Surah 62 Transliteration

Bismillahir Rahmanir Rahim

1. Yusabbihu lilaahi maa fis samaawaati wa maa fil ardil Malikil Quddoosil 'Azeezil Hakeem

2. Huwal lazee ba'asa fil ummiyyeena Rasoolam min hum yatloo 'alayhim aayaatihee wa yuzakeehim wa yu'allimuhumul Kitaaba wal Hikmata wa in kaanoo min qablu lafee dalaalim mubeen

3. Wa aakhareena minhum lammaa yalhaqoo bihim wa huwal 'azeezul hakeem

4. Zaalika fadlullaahi yu'teehi maiy yashaa; wallaahu zul fadlil 'azeem

5. Mathalul lazeena hum milut tawraata thumma lam yahmiloonhaa kamathalil himaari yah milu asfaaraa; bi'sa mathalul qawmil lazeena kaazaboo bi aayaatil laah; wallaahu laa yahdil qawmaz zawlimeen

6. Qul yaa ayyuhal lazeena haadoo in za'amtum annakum awliyaa'u lilaahi min doonin naasi fa ta manna wul mawta in kuntum sawdiqeen

80

7. Wa laa ya ta mannaw nahoo abadam bimaa qaddamat aydeehim; wallaahu 'aleemum biz zawlimeen

8. Qul innal mawtal lazee tafirroona minhu fa innahoo mulaaqeekum thumma turad doona ilaa 'Aalimil Ghaybi wash shahaadati fa yunabbi-ukum bimaa kuntum ta'maloon

9. Yaa ayyuhal lazeena aamanoo izaa noodiya lis-Salaati min yawmil Jumu'ati fas'aw ilaa zikrillaahi wa zarul bai'; zaalikum khayrul lakum in kuntum ta'lamoon

10.   Fa izaa qudiyatis Salaatu fantashiroo fil ardi wabtaghoo min fadlillaahi wazkurul laaha kaseeral la'allakum tuflihoon

11.   Wa izaa ra'aw tijaaratan aw lahwanin faddoo ilaihaa wa tarakooka qaa'imaa; qul maa 'indallaahi khairum minal lahwi wa minat tijaarah; wallaahu khayrur raaziqeen

The Hypocrites

63 Al Munāfiqūn
Early Medinan Period

☞ Introduction

This chapter was revealed about the problems caused by the hypocrite, 'Abdullah ibn Ubayy, and his followers. Ibn Ubayy had already begun plotting against the Prophet from his earliest arrival in Medina, and he looked for every opportunity to sabotage Islam wherever he could.

On the journey back from an expedition against a hostile tribe, and while the Muslim force was encamped, an argument broke out between an Immigrant named Jahjah and a Medinan convert named Sinan ibn Wabrah over whose camel could drink from a well first. The Immigrant hit Sinan and nearly broke his jaw. Some nearby men then began to square off with each other based on their tribal loyalties, and it was only the well-timed intervention of the Prophet that prevented a full-scale brawl. He even told the men that their calls to tribal loyalty were disgusting and that they should give up tribal loyalty as the basis of their allegiance. The original two combatants were also reconciled, though 'Abdullah Ibn Ubayy got angry about the whole affair and looked for an opportunity to cause more trouble like that.

The next evening, while the men were again making camp for the night, Ibn Ubayy approached a gathering of Medinan Muslims and said, "What have you done to yourselves? You let them settle in your land and shared your resources with them. By Allah, if you abandon them, then they'll have to leave and settle in another land." He even suggested that through this tactic they might be able "to throw the beggars," i.e., the Muslims from Mecca, out of their city. He also insulted the Prophet and called him low-class.

One of the Prophet's young companions, Zayd ibn Arqam, heard what Ibn Ubayy said and went to the Prophet to tell him what was happening. 'Umar ibn al-Khattab was upset at the news and asked the Prophet for permission to kill Ibn Ubayy for slander and inciting division. However, the Prophet said, "'Umar, what if people started saying that Muhammad kills his companions? No. Just order the people to start the journey (back to Medina)."

When Ibn Ubayy found out that the Prophet knew about what he had said, he went to him and denied it, claiming that the informant, who was merely a teenager, must have misheard what he said. The Prophet seemed to be convinced by Ibn Ubayy's denial, and this crushed Zayd's spirit, though he said nothing in his defense. The next day the Prophet ordered the expedition to move again, but at an odd time, and so a man went to the Prophet to ask him about it. The Prophet explained that Ibn Ubayy wanted to raise his hand against him. The man, a native of Medina, begged the Prophet to be understanding with Ibn Ubayy, because the people of his city were about to make him their king before the arrival of the Muslims, and he was sore about it.

Before the expedition reentered Medina, however, Ibn Ubayy's own son, a man also named 'Abdullah, stopped his father's camel and refused to let it move until his father apologized for insulting the Prophet. Ibn Ubayy finally relented, and the Prophet asked 'Abdullah to let his father enter the city. (*Ma'ariful Qur'an*) Shortly after the Prophet and his men returned to Medina, this chapter began to be revealed. The Prophet soon sent for Zayd and told him that Allah confirmed that what Zayd had said was true. (*Ibn Hisham, Bukhari*)

In the Name of Allah,
the Compassionate, the Merciful

they obstruct others from the path of Allah. How evil are their actions! [2]

That's because even though they once had faith, they later renounced it, and thus a seal was placed upon their hearts, so that they understand nothing. [3]

When you look at them, their **appearance** impresses you, and when they speak, their influence inclines you to listen.

Yet, even though they (seem confident), they're as weak as propped up sticks – *and they're constantly paranoid of being accused*!

They're the (real) **enemies** (of faith), so watch out for them. Allah's curse be upon them for their careless attitude (towards the truth)! [4]

When the hypocrites come to you, (Muhammad,) they clamor, *"We declare that you are truly the Messenger of Allah,"* but Allah already knows that you're His Messenger, even as He affirms that the hypocrites are a bunch of liars. [1]

They use their public affirmations to disguise (their evil intentions), and that's how

The Boldness of the Arrogant

Background Info... v. 5-6

After 'Abdullah ibn Ubayy refused to go back to the Prophet and repent, despite the insistent urging of so many of his fellows, this passage was revealed. (*Asbab ul-Nuzul*)

When they're told, "*Come, let the Messenger of Allah pray for your forgiveness,*" you see them turning their heads aside and slipping away arrogantly. [5]

It's all the same whether you pray for their forgiveness or not; Allah won't forgive them, for Allah doesn't guide the rebellious. [6]

Withholding Support for Allah's Cause

Background Info... v. 7-8

'Abdullah ibn Ubayy counseled anyone who would listen to him not to give financial support to Muhammad or to any Muslim, under the hope that economic pressure would force the destitute Muslims to either abandon Muhammad or leave the city. His quotes are in these verses. (*Asbab ul-Nuzul*)

They're the ones who say to each other, "*Don't spend your money on any (of the followers) of the Messenger of Allah, for perhaps (one day) they'll leave (him).*"

To Allah belongs the treasures of the heavens and the earth, even though the hypocrites don't realize it. [7]

(Now during the return journey from the campaign against the Banu Mustaliq), they're saying (to each other), "*When we get back to the city, the high class people will throw those beggars out!*"

(Well, they should know that) high **status** belongs only to Allah, His Messenger and the faithful, though the hypocrites don't know it. [8]

Don't Let Worldly Concerns Overtake You

All you who believe! Don't let your money or your children distract you from remembering Allah, for anyone who allows that to happen will be losers (in the end). [9]

Spend something (in charity) out of what We've supplied to you before death should come upon one of you, and he cries out:

"*My Lord! Why didn't you give me a little more time? I would've given (much more) in charity, and I would've been with the righteous!"* [10]

However, no soul will receive from Allah any more time when its **deadline** has come,

and Allah is well-informed of what you're doing. [11]

🗨 Think About It

1. Why was a "seal" placed on the hearts of the hypocrites?

2. Why are hypocrites so influential?

3. Why don't hypocrites like to donate money to charity or help in good causes?

4. Why do families sometimes make us forget Allah?

5. So what advice does this surah give to us, as we approach how to live our lives? Give an example from the text to affirm your argument.

Fill in the Words on the lines below.
Look at the **BOLD** words in the main text to see where they go

Words to Use

Enemies   Appearance   Status   Deadline

---

1. ... no soul will receive from Allah any more time when its _____ has come...

2. They're the (real) _____ (of faith), so watch out for them.

3. When you look at them, their _____ impresses you...

4. (Well, they should know that) high _____ belongs only to Allah...

Complete the Crossword Puzzle Below

(Words can be in any direction, even backwards!)

ACROSS

2. It can distract you from Allah
4. Is well-informed of what you do
6. Allah has done this because they don't care
8. Allah does not guide them
9. Allah owns them all
11. We do not get any more than what we have

DOWN

1. When you are out of time
3. They are as weak as propped up sticks
5. People who are not true
7. Dividing people into different groups
10. A lid to cover something

Arabic Text

١ إِذَا جَاءَكَ الْمُنَافِقُونَ قَالُوا نَشْهَدُ إِنَّكَ لَرَسُولُ اللَّهِ ۗ وَاللَّهُ يَعْلَمُ إِنَّكَ لَرَسُولُهُ وَاللَّهُ يَشْهَدُ إِنَّ الْمُنَافِقِينَ لَكَاذِبُونَ

٢ اتَّخَذُوا أَيْمَانَهُمْ جُنَّةً فَصَدُّوا عَنْ سَبِيلِ اللَّهِ ۚ إِنَّهُمْ سَاءَ مَا كَانُوا يَعْمَلُونَ

٣ ذَٰلِكَ بِأَنَّهُمْ آمَنُوا ثُمَّ كَفَرُوا فَطُبِعَ عَلَىٰ قُلُوبِهِمْ فَهُمْ لَا يَفْقَهُونَ

٤ وَإِذَا رَأَيْتَهُمْ تُعْجِبُكَ أَجْسَامُهُمْ ۖ وَإِنْ يَقُولُوا تَسْمَعْ لِقَوْلِهِمْ ۖ كَأَنَّهُمْ خُشُبٌ مُسَنَّدَةٌ ۖ يَحْسَبُونَ كُلَّ صَيْحَةٍ عَلَيْهِمْ ۚ هُمُ الْعَدُوُّ فَاحْذَرْهُمْ ۚ قَاتَلَهُمُ اللَّهُ ۖ أَنَّىٰ يُؤْفَكُونَ

٥ وَإِذَا قِيلَ لَهُمْ تَعَالَوْا يَسْتَغْفِرْ لَكُمْ رَسُولُ اللَّهِ لَوَّوْا رُءُوسَهُمْ وَرَأَيْتَهُمْ يَصُدُّونَ وَهُمْ مُسْتَكْبِرُونَ

٦ سَوَاءٌ عَلَيْهِمْ أَسْتَغْفَرْتَ لَهُمْ أَمْ لَمْ تَسْتَغْفِرْ لَهُمْ لَنْ يَغْفِرَ اللَّهُ لَهُمْ ۚ إِنَّ اللَّهَ لَا يَهْدِي الْقَوْمَ الْفَاسِقِينَ

٧ هُمُ الَّذِينَ يَقُولُونَ لَا تُنْفِقُوا عَلَىٰ مَنْ عِنْدَ رَسُولِ اللَّهِ حَتَّىٰ يَنْفَضُّوا ۗ وَلِلَّهِ خَزَائِنُ السَّمَاوَاتِ وَالْأَرْضِ وَلَٰكِنَّ الْمُنَافِقِينَ لَا يَفْقَهُونَ

٨ يَقُولُونَ لَئِنْ رَجَعْنَا إِلَى الْمَدِينَةِ لَيُخْرِجَنَّ الْأَعَزُّ مِنْهَا الْأَذَلَّ ۚ وَلِلَّهِ الْعِزَّةُ وَلِرَسُولِهِ وَلِلْمُؤْمِنِينَ وَلَٰكِنَّ الْمُنَافِقِينَ لَا يَعْلَمُونَ

٩ يَا أَيُّهَا الَّذِينَ آمَنُوا لَا تُلْهِكُمْ أَمْوَالُكُمْ وَلَا أَوْلَادُكُمْ عَنْ ذِكْرِ اللَّهِ ۚ وَمَنْ يَفْعَلْ ذَٰلِكَ فَأُولَٰئِكَ هُمُ الْخَاسِرُونَ

١٠ وَأَنْفِقُوا مِنْ مَا رَزَقْنَاكُمْ مِنْ قَبْلِ أَنْ يَأْتِيَ أَحَدَكُمُ الْمَوْتُ فَيَقُولَ رَبِّ لَوْلَا أَخَّرْتَنِي إِلَىٰ أَجَلٍ قَرِيبٍ فَأَصَّدَّقَ وَأَكُنْ مِنَ الصَّالِحِينَ

١١ وَلَنْ يُؤَخِّرَ اللَّهُ نَفْسًا إِذَا جَاءَ أَجَلُهَا ۚ وَاللَّهُ خَبِيرٌ بِمَا تَعْمَلُونَ

Surah 63 Transliteration

Bismillahir Rahmanir Rahim

1. Izaa jaa-akal munaafiqoona qawloo nashhadu innaka la rasoolullaah; wallaahu ya'lamu innaka la rasooluhoo wallaahu yash hadu innal munaafiqeena lakaaziboon

2. Ittakhazoo aymaanahum junnatan fasaddoo 'an sabeelillaah; innahum saa'a maa kaanoo ya'maloon

3. Zaalika bi annahum aamanoo thumma kafaroo fatubi'a 'alaa quloobihim fahum laa yaf qahoon

4. Wa izaa ra aytahum tu'jibuka ajsaamuhum wa iy yaqooloo tasma' liqawlihim kaannahum khushubum musan nadah; yah saboona kulla sayhatin 'alayhim; humul 'aduwwu fahzarhum; qaatalahumullaahu annaa yu'fakoon

5. Wa izaa qeela lahum ta'aalaw yastaghfir lakum rasoolullaahi lawwaw ru'oo sahum wa ra-aytahum yasuddoona wa hum mustakbiroon

6. Sawaa-un 'alayhim as taghfarta lahum am lam tastaghfir lahum laiy yaghfirallaahu lahum; innallaaha laa yah dil qawmal faasiqeen

7. Humul lazeena yaqooloona laa tunfiqoo 'alaa man 'inda Rasoolillaahi hatta yanfaddoo; wa lillaahi khazaa' inus samaawaati wal ardi wa laakinnal munaafiqeena la yaf qahoon

8. Yaqooloona la'ir raja'naa ilal madeenati la yukhrijanal a'azzu minhal azall; wa lillaahil 'izzatu wa li Rasoolihee wa lilmu'mineena wa laakinnal munaafiqeena laa ya'lamoon

9. Yaa ayyuhal lazeena aamanoo la tulhikum amwaalukum wa laa awlaadukum 'anzikrillaah; wa may-yaf'al zaalika fa-ulaa-ika humul khaasiroon

10. Wa anfiqoo mim maa razaq naakum min qabli aiy-ya'tiya ahadakumul mawtu fa yaqoola rabbi law laa akhartanee ilaa ajalin qareebin fa assaddaqa wa akum minas sawliheen

11. Wa laiy yu 'akhkhiral laahu nafsan izaa jaa'a ajaluhaa; wallahu khabeerum bimaa ta'maloon

Varied Fortune

64 Al Taghābūn
Early Medinan Period

☞ Introduction

This is something of a transitional chapter that was revealed just after the migration to Medina in the year 622. For this reason, it resembles a Meccan chapter in its subject matter, though its addressing of hardships in verses 11-18 shows that its ultimate purpose was to provide the desperate Muslim refugees with some words of advice on how to view their plight and also on how to rise above it. It cannot be overappreciated how difficult it is for people to leave their homes and cities under a barrage of persecution, and it was extremely arduous and stressful upon the Muslim faithful.

In the Name of Allah,
the Compassionate, the Merciful

Whatever is within the heavens and on earth reflects the glory of Allah. All dominion and praise belong to Him, and He has power over all things. [1]

He's the One Who created you, and among you are some who reject (Allah) and some who believe. Allah is watching whatever you do. [2]

He created the heavens and the earth for a true **purpose**. He crafted you, and you've been crafted well, and to Him is the journey's end. [3]

He knows what's in the heavens and on the earth, and He knows what you hide and what you show, for Allah knows the secrets of the heart. [4]

Haven't you encountered the tales of all the faithless (nations) who came before you? They suffered the consequences of their actions, and they're going to have a painful punishment. [5]

That's because whenever messengers went to them with clear evidence (of the truth, they scoffed at it), saying, *"How can some regular person show us the way?"*

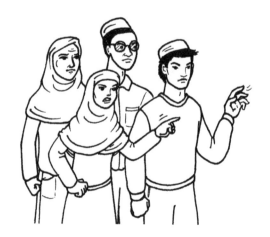

So they rejected (the message) and turned away. Allah had no need of them, for Allah is self-sufficient and is already being praised. [6]

Those who cover over (their awareness of Allah) assume that they're never going to be resurrected.

Say to them, "*For sure! By my Lord, you're going to be resurrected, and then you'll be made to understand (the meaning of) all that you did. That's easy for Allah to do.*" [7]

So believe in Allah and His Messenger and in the light that We've sent down, for Allah is well-informed of everything you do. [8]

The day when He gathers you all together for the Day of Gathering - that will be a day of varied fortune. Whoever believed in Allah and did what was **morally** right will have their faults erased by Him.

He'll admit them into gardens beneath which rivers flow, and there they'll remain **forever**. That's the greatest success! [9]

But those who rejected (the truth) and denied Our signs will be companions of the Fire, and that's where they're going to stay, and that's the worst of all destinations! [10]

How Should We Think about Life's Challenges?

No catastrophe can ever happen except with Allah's permission. Whoever believes in Allah, He will then guide his heart, for Allah knows about everything. [11]

So obey Allah and obey His Messenger, though if anyone turns aside, Our Messenger's only duty is to convey (the message) clearly. [12]

Allah: there is no god but He, and the faithful should trust in Allah! [13]

Remain True to the Way

> **Background Info... v. 14-16**
>
> This passage was revealed about people who converted to Islam in Mecca and who wanted to migrate to Medina, but their unconverted wives or husbands and children refused to go with them, and so the converts stayed in Mecca. Later on, when they finally did migrate with their families, they found that those who had arrived before them had gained much more knowledge of the religion.
>
> Such people then spent much more of their time in the masjid or doing charity or other good deeds. Their families would then scold them, complain and make them feel guilty for going out and learning, preaching, teaching, etc. (*Asbab ul-Nuzul*)

> Some commentators say this verse is specifically about the case of a companion named 'Auf ibn Malik Ashja'i, who always volunteered whenever there was a call to arms. His wife and children would complain to him, saying, "And in whose care are you going to leave us?" (*Ma'ariful Qur'an*)
>
> The Muslims are asked to be patient and to forgive their families, however, for perhaps their fears are real to them. In a wider sense, this is general advice to be patient with one's family when they seem to be less than supportive. It may be just a test for us to see if we are truly patient and wise.

All you who believe! There are potential adversaries for you among your spouses and children, so watch out!

However, if you overlook (their faults), gloss over (their shortcomings) and forgive them, (know that) Allah is forgiving and merciful. [14]

Your wealth and your children may be a test for you, but the greatest reward is in Allah's presence! [15]

The Most Beautiful Loan

Be mindful (of your duty) to Allah to the best of your **ability**, listen and obey, and spend (in charity) for your own good. Whoever saves himself from the greed of his own soul will be victorious. [16]

If you lend a beautiful loan to Allah, He will double it (to your benefit) and forgive you (your sins), for Allah is appreciative and forbearing. [17]

He knows what's beyond perception, as well as what's plainly visible, (for He is) the Powerful and Wise. [18]

Think About It

1. Why were nations of the past punished with disasters, invasions and being destroyed?

2. In verse 7, what is one of the purposes of resurrection, and why is that important?

3. Why will people have 'varied fortune' on the Day of Gathering?

4. Verse 14 warns that there are potential enemies in our own families. Explain why this can be the case, and use evidence from real life or the background information.

5. Why is it important to be patient and forgiving with family members who might be against us?

Fill in the Words on the lines below.
Look at the **BOLD** words in the main text to see where they go

Words to Use

Purpose   Morally   Ability   Forever

---

1. Whoever believed in Allah and did what was _____ right will have their faults erased by Him.

2. He'll admit them into gardens beneath which rivers flow, and there they'll remain _____.

3. He created the heavens and the earth for a true _____.

4. Be mindful (of your duty) to Allah to the best of your _____, listen and obey, and spend (in charity) for your own good.

Complete the Crossword Puzzle Below

(Words can be in any direction, even backwards!)

ACROSS

4. Where good people go
5. Only by Allah's permission
7. Where bad people go
8. They should trust in Allah
9. One of Allah's attributes

DOWN

1. Allah will erase these from believers
2. Allah is doing this
3. The Day of
6. What people do who reject the prophets
8. Relatives who were bad
10. Give this beautiful thing to Allah

Arabic Text

بِسْمِ اللَّهِ الرَّحْمَٰنِ الرَّحِيمِ

١ يُسَبِّحُ لِلَّهِ مَا فِي السَّمَاوَاتِ وَمَا فِي الْأَرْضِ ۖ لَهُ الْمُلْكُ وَلَهُ الْحَمْدُ ۖ وَهُوَ عَلَىٰ كُلِّ شَيْءٍ قَدِيرٌ

٢ هُوَ الَّذِي خَلَقَكُمْ فَمِنْكُمْ كَافِرٌ وَمِنْكُمْ مُؤْمِنٌ ۚ وَاللَّهُ بِمَا تَعْمَلُونَ بَصِيرٌ

٣ خَلَقَ السَّمَاوَاتِ وَالْأَرْضَ بِالْحَقِّ وَصَوَّرَكُمْ فَأَحْسَنَ صُوَرَكُمْ ۖ وَإِلَيْهِ الْمَصِيرُ

٤ يَعْلَمُ مَا فِي السَّمَاوَاتِ وَالْأَرْضِ وَيَعْلَمُ مَا تُسِرُّونَ وَمَا تُعْلِنُونَ ۚ وَاللَّهُ عَلِيمٌ بِذَاتِ الصُّدُورِ

٥ أَلَمْ يَأْتِكُمْ نَبَأُ الَّذِينَ كَفَرُوا مِنْ قَبْلُ فَذَاقُوا وَبَالَ أَمْرِهِمْ وَلَهُمْ عَذَابٌ أَلِيمٌ

٦ ذَٰلِكَ بِأَنَّهُ كَانَتْ تَأْتِيهِمْ رُسُلُهُمْ بِالْبَيِّنَاتِ فَقَالُوا أَبَشَرٌ يَهْدُونَنَا فَكَفَرُوا وَتَوَلَّوْا ۚ وَاسْتَغْنَى اللَّهُ ۚ وَاللَّهُ غَنِيٌّ حَمِيدٌ

٧ زَعَمَ الَّذِينَ كَفَرُوا أَنْ لَنْ يُبْعَثُوا ۚ قُلْ بَلَىٰ وَرَبِّي لَتُبْعَثُنَّ ثُمَّ لَتُنَبَّؤُنَّ بِمَا عَمِلْتُمْ ۚ وَذَٰلِكَ عَلَى اللَّهِ يَسِيرٌ

٨ فَآمِنُوا بِاللَّهِ وَرَسُولِهِ وَالنُّورِ الَّذِي أَنْزَلْنَا ۚ وَاللَّهُ بِمَا تَعْمَلُونَ خَبِيرٌ

٩ يَوْمَ يَجْمَعُكُمْ لِيَوْمِ الْجَمْعِ ۖ ذَٰلِكَ يَوْمُ التَّغَابُنِ ۗ وَمَنْ يُؤْمِنْ بِاللَّهِ وَيَعْمَلْ صَالِحًا يُكَفِّرْ عَنْهُ سَيِّئَاتِهِ وَيُدْخِلْهُ جَنَّاتٍ تَجْرِي مِنْ تَحْتِهَا الْأَنْهَارُ خَالِدِينَ فِيهَا أَبَدًا ۚ ذَٰلِكَ الْفَوْزُ الْعَظِيمُ

١٠ وَالَّذِينَ كَفَرُوا وَكَذَّبُوا بِآيَاتِنَا أُولَٰئِكَ أَصْحَابُ النَّارِ خَالِدِينَ فِيهَا وَبِئْسَ الْمَصِيرُ

١١ مَا أَصَابَ مِنْ مُصِيبَةٍ إِلَّا بِإِذْنِ اللَّهِ ۗ وَمَنْ يُؤْمِنْ بِاللَّهِ يَهْدِ قَلْبَهُ وَاللَّهُ بِكُلِّ شَيْءٍ عَلِيمٌ

١٢ وَأَطِيعُوا اللَّهَ وَأَطِيعُوا الرَّسُولَ ۚ فَإِنْ تَوَلَّيْتُمْ فَإِنَّمَا عَلَىٰ رَسُولِنَا الْبَلَاغُ الْمُبِينُ

١٣ اللَّهُ لَا إِلَٰهَ إِلَّا هُوَ ۚ وَعَلَى اللَّهِ فَلْيَتَوَكَّلِ الْمُؤْمِنُونَ

١٤ يَا أَيُّهَا الَّذِينَ آمَنُوا إِنَّ مِنْ أَزْوَاجِكُمْ وَأَوْلَادِكُمْ عَدُوًّا لَكُمْ فَاحْذَرُوهُمْ ۚ وَإِنْ تَعْفُوا وَتَصْفَحُوا وَتَغْفِرُوا فَإِنَّ اللَّهَ غَفُورٌ رَحِيمٌ

١٥ إِنَّمَا أَمْوَالُكُمْ وَأَوْلَادُكُمْ فِتْنَةٌ ۚ وَاللَّهُ عِنْدَهُ أَجْرٌ عَظِيمٌ

١٦ فَاتَّقُوا اللَّهَ مَا اسْتَطَعْتُمْ وَاسْمَعُوا وَأَطِيعُوا وَأَنْفِقُوا خَيْرًا لِأَنْفُسِكُمْ ۗ وَمَنْ يُوقَ شُحَّ نَفْسِهِ فَأُولَٰئِكَ هُمُ الْمُفْلِحُونَ

١٧ إِنْ تُقْرِضُوا اللَّهَ قَرْضًا حَسَنًا يُضَاعِفْهُ لَكُمْ وَيَغْفِرْ لَكُمْ ۚ وَاللَّهُ شَكُورٌ حَلِيمٌ

١٨ عَالِمُ الْغَيْبِ وَالشَّهَادَةِ الْعَزِيزُ الْحَكِيمُ

Surah 64 Transliteration

Bismillahir Rahmanir Rahim

1. Yusabbihu lillaahi maa fis samaawaati wa maa fil ardi lahul mulku wa lahul hamd, wa Huwa 'alaa kulli shaiy 'in Qadeer

2. Huwal lazee khalaqakum faminkum kaafirun wa min kum mu-min ; wallaahu bimaa ta'maloona Baseer

3. Khalaqas samaawaati wal arda bilhaqqi wa sawwarakum fa ahsana suwarakum wa ilayhil maseer

4. Ya'lamu maa fis samaawaati wal ardi wa ya'lamu maa tusirroona wa maa tu'linoon; wallaahu 'Aleemum bizaatis sudoor

5. Alam ya'tikum naba'ul lazeena kafaroo min qablu fazaaqoo wabaala amrihim wa lahum 'azaabun aleem

6. Zaalika bi annahoo kaanat ta'teehim Rusuluhum bilbaiyinaati faqaaloo a basharui yah doonanaa fakafaroo wa tawallaw; wastaghnallaah; wallaahu ghaniyyun hameed

7. Za'amal lazeena kafaroo al-lany yub'asoo; qul balaa wa rabbee latub'asunna thumma latunabba'unna bimaa 'amiltum; wa zaalika 'alallaahi yaseer

8. Fa aaminoo billaahi wa rasoolihee wannooril lazee anzalnaa; wallaahu bima ta'maloona khabeer

9. Yawma yajma'ukum li yawmil jam'i zaalika yawmut taghaabun; wa maiy-yumim billaahi wa ya'mal saalihany yukaffir 'anhu sayyi aatihee wa yudkhilhu jannaatin tajree min tahtihal anhaaru khaalideena feehaa abadaa; zaalikal fawzul 'azeem

10. Wallazeena kafaroo wa kazzaboo bi ayaatinaa ulaa-ika as haabun naar. khaalideena feehaa wa bi-sal maseer

11. Maa asaaba mim musee batin illaa bi-iznillaah; wa maiy yu'mim billaahi yahdi qalbah; wallaahu bikulli shaiy'in Aleem

12. Wa atee'ul laaha wa atee'ur Rasool; fa in tawallaytum fa innamaa 'alaa Rasoolinal balaaghul mubeen

13. Allaahu laa ilaaha illaa Hoo; wa 'alallaahi falyata wakkalil mu'minoon

14. Yaa ayyuhal lazeena aamanoo inna min azwaaji kum wa awlaadikum 'aduwwal lakum fahzaroohum; wa in ta'foo wa tasfahoo wa taghfiroo fa innallaaha ghafoorur Raheem

15. Innamaa amwaalukum wa awlaadukum fitnah; wallaahu 'indahoo ajrun 'azeem

16. Fattaqul laaha mastata'tum wasma'oo wa atee'oo wa anfiqoo khayral li anfusikum; wa maiy-yooqa shuh ha nafsihee fa-ulaa-ika humul muf lihoon

17. In tuqridullaaha qardan hasananaiy yudaayfhu lakum wa yaghfir lakum; wallaahu Shakoorun Haleem

18. 'Aalimul-Ghaybi wash-shahaadatil 'Azeezul Hakeem

Divorce

65 At-Talāq
Middle Medinan Period

☞ Introduction

This chapter was revealed sometime after the rules about divorce were announced in chapter two. Marriage and divorce are facts of life. It happened that some divorces occurred in the community, most notably that of 'Abdullah, the son of 'Umar ibn al-Khattab, who divorced his wife while she was on her monthly. (It is forbidden to divorce women while they are in that state.)

The Prophet ordered him to take her back and start the divorce process over again. In addition, some people were misunderstanding the divorce rules mentioned in chapter two, specifically in verses 228-234. This new chapter was sent as something of an add-on to further clarify and explain the rules governing marriage and divorce.

In the Name of Allah,
the Compassionate, the Merciful

Prophet! When (any of you men) intend to divorce women, (you must) divorce them after their waiting periods (are complete) – and count them accurately. Be mindful of Allah, your Lord!

(During the waiting period, men) must not drive (their wives) from their homes or (make them feel) they must **leave**, except in cases involving clear indecency.

These are the rules set by Allah. Anyone who disregards the rules set by Allah brings harm only upon himself. You don't know if Allah might change your situation (for the better). [1]

Then, when they've fulfilled their appointed time, either retain (your spouses) in fairness, or let them go in fairness.

Choose two people among you who are known for their evenhandedness as witnesses, and present the case (to them, knowing that you are also) before Allah.

This is how those who believe in Allah and the Last Day are instructed.

Whoever is mindful of Allah will be shown a way out (of distress), [2] and He'll provide for them from where they least expect it.

Whoever relies upon Allah (should know that) Allah is enough for him. Allah achieves His objective, and Allah has determined the course of all things. [3]

An Exemption on Clothing Restrictions for Elderly Women

> **Background Info... v. 4-5**
>
> Ubayy ibn K'ab said to the Prophet, "After the verses in the Chapter of the Cow concerning the waiting period were revealed, some people in Medina said that there were still some women whose waiting periods were not mentioned, specifically the old, the young and the pregnant (who might be left widows before their baby is born)." This passage was revealed in response. (*Asbab ul-Nuzul*)

Now as for those women who are too old to menstruate or who don't have it for other reasons, their waiting period, to dispel any doubts, is three months.

Any woman who is pregnant will wait for the birth (of her child, and then her waiting period will end). Whoever is mindful of Allah (should know that) He will make his affair an easy one. [4]

This is the command of Allah that He's sending down to you. Whoever is **mindful** of Allah will have his shortcomings erased and his reward increased. [5]

Support (women in their waiting period) in your same standard of living, according to your financial ability, and don't harass them in the hopes of making their situation worse.

If they're pregnant, then pay all their **expenses** until they give birth.

Then afterwards, if they wean (the infant) by themselves, then compensate them, and consult with each other fairly (on issues related to the child).

If (nursing the baby) is a hardship for (any of) you (women), then (the ex-husband must pay for) the child to be weaned by a wet-nurse. [6]

Let the wealthy spend according to their means, and let those of more modest means do likewise.

Allah doesn't burden any soul beyond what He's given it (to work with), and Allah will soon make things easier. [7]

Take the Lesson While You Can

How many settlements rebelled against the command of their Lord and His messengers, (despite the fact) that We called them on it and thereafter punished them with unprecedented retribution? [8]

They felt the serious consequences of their actions, and the final result of their efforts brought about their own fall. [9]

Allah has prepared a stern punishment for them, so be mindful of Allah, all you reasonable people who believe, for Allah has sent a reminder down to you: [10] a messenger who recites the clearly evident verses of Allah, so he can lead the believers who do what's morally right from darkness into light.

Whoever believes in Allah and does what's morally right will be admitted by Him into gardens beneath which rivers flow to live within forever, and Allah will give them an excellent share! [11]

Allah is the One Who created the seven-layered skies and the similarly ordered (structure of the) earth.

Through them **flows** His command, so you can know that Allah has power over all things and that Allah has inclusive knowledge of everything. [12]

1. Why do you think so many rules are placed on those men who want to divorce their wives?

2. So the waiting period is to know if a woman is going to have a baby, because it might make the husband think again about wanting a divorce. What does this say about how Islam views the importance of the family?

3. From verses 1-7, would you say these are more beneficial rules for the protection of women or men? Give evidence from the text to support your argument.

4. Before punishing any corrupt civilization in the distant past, in what ways did Allah try to help them improve first?

5. Verse 12 mentions that the skies and the earth are well-ordered and structured. Look up the names of the layers of the earth and write them below.

Fill in the Words on the lines below.
Look at the **BOLD** words in the main text to see where they go

Words to Use

Leave   Mindful   Expenses   Flows

---

1. (During the waiting period, men) must not drive (their wives) from their homes or (make them feel) they must _____...

2. Through them _____ His command, so you can know that Allah has power over all things

3. Whoever is _____ of Allah will have his shortcomings erased and his reward increased.

4. If they're pregnant, then pay all their _____ until they give birth.

Complete the Crossword Puzzle Below

(Words can be in any direction, even backwards!)

ACROSS

4. When a couple separates
6. A time period of this before divorce
8. the kind of punishment evildoers will get
10. The ex-husband must support
11. Men must pay for their wives
12. Allah brings the sincere into this
14. Allah achieves His

DOWN

1. Allah will not burden it more than it can bear
2. Clear signs or messages from Allah
3. Have consequences
4. Allah takes the sincere out of this
5. Called to mediate at the time of divorce
6. Must be supported
7. Day
9. Set by Allah
13. They flow in Paradise

Arabic Text

بِسْمِ اللَّهِ الرَّحْمَٰنِ الرَّحِيمِ

١ يَا أَيُّهَا النَّبِيُّ إِذَا طَلَّقْتُمُ النِّسَاءَ فَطَلِّقُوهُنَّ لِعِدَّتِهِنَّ وَأَحْصُوا الْعِدَّةَ وَاتَّقُوا اللَّهَ رَبَّكُمْ ۖ لَا تُخْرِجُوهُنَّ مِنْ بُيُوتِهِنَّ وَلَا يَخْرُجْنَ إِلَّا أَنْ يَأْتِينَ بِفَاحِشَةٍ مُبَيِّنَةٍ ۚ وَتِلْكَ حُدُودُ اللَّهِ ۚ وَمَنْ يَتَعَدَّ حُدُودَ اللَّهِ فَقَدْ ظَلَمَ نَفْسَهُ ۚ لَا تَدْرِي لَعَلَّ اللَّهَ يُحْدِثُ بَعْدَ ذَٰلِكَ أَمْرًا

٢ فَإِذَا بَلَغْنَ أَجَلَهُنَّ فَأَمْسِكُوهُنَّ بِمَعْرُوفٍ أَوْ فَارِقُوهُنَّ بِمَعْرُوفٍ وَأَشْهِدُوا ذَوَيْ عَدْلٍ مِنْكُمْ وَأَقِيمُوا الشَّهَادَةَ لِلَّهِ ۚ ذَٰلِكُمْ يُوعَظُ بِهِ مَنْ كَانَ يُؤْمِنُ بِاللَّهِ وَالْيَوْمِ الْآخِرِ ۚ وَمَنْ يَتَّقِ اللَّهَ يَجْعَلْ لَهُ مَخْرَجًا

٣ وَيَرْزُقْهُ مِنْ حَيْثُ لَا يَحْتَسِبُ ۚ وَمَنْ يَتَوَكَّلْ عَلَى اللَّهِ فَهُوَ حَسْبُهُ ۚ إِنَّ اللَّهَ بَالِغُ أَمْرِهِ ۚ قَدْ جَعَلَ اللَّهُ لِكُلِّ شَيْءٍ قَدْرًا

٤ وَاللَّائِي يَئِسْنَ مِنَ الْمَحِيضِ مِنْ نِسَائِكُمْ إِنِ ارْتَبْتُمْ فَعِدَّتُهُنَّ ثَلَاثَةُ أَشْهُرٍ وَاللَّائِي لَمْ يَحِضْنَ ۚ وَأُولَاتُ الْأَحْمَالِ أَجَلُهُنَّ أَنْ يَضَعْنَ حَمْلَهُنَّ ۚ وَمَنْ يَتَّقِ اللَّهَ يَجْعَلْ لَهُ مِنْ أَمْرِهِ يُسْرًا

٥ ذَٰلِكَ أَمْرُ اللَّهِ أَنْزَلَهُ إِلَيْكُمْ ۚ وَمَنْ يَتَّقِ اللَّهَ يُكَفِّرْ عَنْهُ سَيِّئَاتِهِ وَيُعْظِمْ لَهُ أَجْرًا

٦ أَسْكِنُوهُنَّ مِنْ حَيْثُ سَكَنْتُمْ مِنْ وُجْدِكُمْ وَلَا تُضَارُّوهُنَّ لِتُضَيِّقُوا عَلَيْهِنَّ ۚ وَإِنْ كُنَّ أُولَاتِ حَمْلٍ فَأَنْفِقُوا عَلَيْهِنَّ حَتَّىٰ يَضَعْنَ حَمْلَهُنَّ ۚ فَإِنْ أَرْضَعْنَ لَكُمْ فَآتُوهُنَّ أُجُورَهُنَّ ۖ وَأْتَمِرُوا بَيْنَكُمْ بِمَعْرُوفٍ ۖ وَإِنْ تَعَاسَرْتُمْ فَسَتُرْضِعُ لَهُ أُخْرَىٰ

٧ لِيُنْفِقْ ذُو سَعَةٍ مِنْ سَعَتِهِ ۖ وَمَنْ قُدِرَ عَلَيْهِ رِزْقُهُ فَلْيُنْفِقْ مِمَّا آتَاهُ اللَّهُ ۚ لَا يُكَلِّفُ اللَّهُ نَفْسًا إِلَّا مَا آتَاهَا ۚ سَيَجْعَلُ اللَّهُ بَعْدَ عُسْرٍ يُسْرًا

٨ وَكَأَيِّنْ مِنْ قَرْيَةٍ عَتَتْ عَنْ أَمْرِ رَبِّهَا وَرُسُلِهِ فَحَاسَبْنَاهَا حِسَابًا شَدِيدًا وَعَذَّبْنَاهَا عَذَابًا نُكْرًا

٩ فَذَاقَتْ وَبَالَ أَمْرِهَا وَكَانَ عَاقِبَةُ أَمْرِهَا خُسْرًا

١٠ أَعَدَّ اللَّهُ لَهُمْ عَذَابًا شَدِيدًا ۖ فَاتَّقُوا اللَّهَ يَا أُولِي الْأَلْبَابِ الَّذِينَ آمَنُوا قَدْ أَنْزَلَ اللَّهُ إِلَيْكُمْ ذِكْرًا

١١ رَسُولًا يَتْلُو عَلَيْكُمْ آيَاتِ اللَّهِ مُبَيِّنَاتٍ لِيُخْرِجَ الَّذِينَ آمَنُوا وَعَمِلُوا الصَّالِحَاتِ مِنَ الظُّلُمَاتِ إِلَى النُّورِ ۚ وَمَنْ يُؤْمِنْ بِاللَّهِ وَيَعْمَلْ صَالِحًا يُدْخِلْهُ جَنَّاتٍ تَجْرِي مِنْ تَحْتِهَا الْأَنْهَارُ خَالِدِينَ فِيهَا أَبَدًا ۖ قَدْ أَحْسَنَ اللَّهُ لَهُ رِزْقًا

١٢ اللَّهُ الَّذِي خَلَقَ سَبْعَ سَمَاوَاتٍ وَمِنَ الْأَرْضِ مِثْلَهُنَّ يَتَنَزَّلُ الْأَمْرُ بَيْنَهُنَّ لِتَعْلَمُوا أَنَّ اللَّهَ عَلَىٰ كُلِّ شَيْءٍ قَدِيرٌ وَأَنَّ اللَّهَ قَدْ أَحَاطَ بِكُلِّ شَيْءٍ عِلْمًا

Surah 65 Transliteration

Bismillahir Rahmanir Rahim

1. Yaa ayyuhan nabiyyu izaa tallaqtummun nisaa'a fatalliqoohunna li'iddatihinna wa ahsul'iddah. Wattaqul laaha rabbakum; laa tukhri joohunna mim bu-yootihinna wa laa yakhrujna illaa aiy ya'teema bifaahishatim mubayyinah; wa tilka hudoodullaah; wa maiy yata'adda hudoodal laahi faqad zalama nafsah; laa tadree la'allallaaha yuhdisu ba'dazaalika amraa

2. Fa izaa balaghna ajalahunna fa amsikoohunna bima'roofin aw faariqoohunna bima'roofin wa ashhidoo zaway 'adlim minkum wa aqeemush shahaadata lillaah; zaalikum yoo'azu bihee man kaana yu'minu billaahi wal yawmil aakhir; wa maiy yattaqil laaha yaj'al lahoo makhrajaa

3. Wa yarzuqhu min haythu laa yahtasib; wa many yatawakkal 'alal laahi fahuwa husbuh; innal laaha baalighu amrih; qad ja'alal laahu likulli shay'in qadraa

110

4. Wallaa'ee ya'isna minal maheedi min nisaa 'ikum inir tabtum fa'iddatu hunna thalaathatu ash hurin wallaa'ee lam yahidn; wa ulaatul ah maali ajalu hunna aiy yada'na hamlahun; wa maiy yattaqil laaha yaj'al lahoo min amrihee yusraa

5. Zaalika amrul laahi anzalahoo ilaykum; wa maiy yattaqil laaha yukaffir 'anhu saiyi-aatihee wa yu'zim lahoo ajraa

6. Askinoohunna min haythu sakantum min wujdikum wa laa tudaarroohunna litudaiyiqoo 'alayhin; wa in kunna ulaati hamlin fa anfiqoo 'alayhinna hattaa yada'na hamlahunn; fa-in 'arda'na lakum fa aatoo hunna ujoorahun; wa'tamiroo baynakum bi ma'roofin wa in ta'aasartum fasaturdi'u lahoo ukhraa

7. Liyunfiq zoo sa'atim min sa'atih; wa man qudira 'alayhi rizquhoo fal yunfiq mimmaa aataahullaah; laa yukalliful laahu nafsan illaa maa aataahaa; sa yaj'alul laahu ba'da'usriy yusraa

8. Wa ka ayyim min qaryatin 'atat 'an amri Rabbihaa wa Rusulihee fahaa sabnaahaa hisaaban shadeedan wa 'azzab naahaa 'azaaban nukraa

9. Fazaaqat wabbala amrihaa wa kaana 'aaqibatu amrihaa khusraa

10.   A'ad dallaahu lahum 'azaaban shadeedan fattaqul laaha yaa ulil albaab, allazeena aammanoo; qad anzalal laahu ilaykum zikraa

11.   Rasoolaiy yatloo 'alaykum aayaatil laahi mubaiyinaatil liyukh rijal lazeena aamanoo wa 'amilus saalihaati minaz zulumaati ilan noor; wa maiy yu'min billaahi wa ya'mal saalihaiy yudkhilhu jannaatin tajree min tahtihal anhaaru khaalideena feehaa abadaa qad ahsanal laahu lahoo rizqaa

12.   Allaahul lazee khalaq Sab'a Samaawaatin wa minal ardi mislahunna yatanazzalul amru bayna hunna lita'lamoo annal laaha 'alaa kulli shai-in Qadeerun wa annal laaha qad ahaata bikulli shai-in 'ilmaa

Prohibition

66 At-Tahreem
Middle Medinan Period

☞ Introduction

The Prophet's beloved wife Khadijah had passed away in Mecca, and for while the Prophet lived alone. His companions urged him to marry again, and the Prophet did so and wound up marrying many poor widows but also some women who had influence with their tribes or clans. Most of those marriages happened after he and the Muslims moved to Medina.

The wives of the Prophet are called the "Mothers of the Believers" because they were leaders in the community. Even though the wives of the Prophet were good examples for the believers to follow, they were still only human, and there were times when there was tension among the Prophet's wives, and sometimes the tension affected the Prophet.

During one of those rare times, the Prophet felt like some of them were secretly talking about each other and even about him and this situation made the Prophet feel sad and frustrated. Each wife had her own apartment, and sometimes when the Prophet visited with one of them or another he would find tension and things that worried him. Angel Gabriel even told the Prophet about what was going on.

The Prophet tried talking to his wives for a while, asking them to be nice to him and be sincere to Allah. When that didn't work, he moved out of his apartment and into the second floor apartment of one of his companions. He lived there for a month.

This chapter was revealed to help the Prophet offer his wives a divorce if they wanted to leave him, and it promised them a good amount of money if they wanted to do that so they could make a decision not based on fears of being poor. None of the wives of the Prophet wanted to divorce him, so 'Umar ibn al-Khattab went to the Prophet and asked him if he was planning to divorce his wives. The Prophet said that he was not, and harmony returned to his home life. (This entire episode is an example of the advice given in the Qur'an in verse 4:34.)

In the Name of Allah,
the Compassionate, the Merciful

O Prophet! Why would you forbid yourself from something that Allah has allowed for you?

Are you thinking that this is what you have to do to please your spouses? Allah is forgiving and merciful! [1]

Allah has already given you a required method to cancel your (hasty) **promises**. Allah is the protector of you all, and He is the Knowing and the Wise. [2]

When the Prophet told something in **confidence** to one wife, she told it to another, and Allah made this known to him. Then he had (to tell others about the matter), while leaving some of its (details) vague.

113

When he confronted her (about her having told the secret), she exclaimed, "*Who told you that (I told someone else)?*"

"*I was informed,*" he said, "*by the Knowing and the Well-Informed.*" [3]

Both of you, (the wife who told the secret and the one to whom she told it), should turn to Allah in repentance, if your hearts lead you to do it.

If you try to defend each other against (the Prophet, know that) his protector is Allah, even as is Jibra'il, every righteous believer and the very angels themselves, who will all defend him. [4]

(Wives of the Prophet), if he were to divorce you all, it just might be that Allah would provide him with wives who are much better than you, who are surrendered (to Allah), who believe, who are devout, penitent, dedicated to (Allah's) service and who are outgoing (in spreading the faith), whether previously married or not. [5]

Save Your Family

All you who believe! Save yourselves and your families from a fire whose fuel is men and the stone (of idols), over which are appointed strict and severe angels who don't hesitate from thoroughly carrying out the commands they receive from Allah, and they do whatever they're commanded. [6]

(The angels will scold the inmates of Hell, saying,) "*All you who covered over (your awareness of the truth)! Make no more excuses today! You're not being punished as much as you're being **repaid** for what you did!*" [7]

Be True to the Cause

All you who believe! Turn to Allah in repentance with sincere remorse. It may be that your Lord will erase some of your sins and admit you into gardens beneath which rivers flow.

On that day, Allah will shield the Prophet and the believers (who followed) him from any humiliation.

The light (of their purity) will shine before them and from their right hands, and they will say:

"*Our Lord, perfect our* **light** *and forgive us, for You have power over all things.*" [8]

O Prophet! Struggle hard against the faithless and the hypocrites; be firm against them, for their final home is in Hellfire, the worst destination! [9]

For the faithless, Allah points out the example of the wife of Nuh and the wife of Lut. They were under (the care) of two of our righteous servants; yet, each betrayed (her husband).

Their (association with their husbands) did them no good against Allah, for they're going to be told, "*Enter the Fire along with all those who have to enter!*" [10]

For the believers, Allah points out the example of Pharaoh's wife who had prayed, "*My Lord, prepare for me a house in the Garden near to You. Save me from the (evil) deeds of (my husband), the pharaoh, and save me from the wrongdoers.*" [11]

(Yet another example) is that of Maryam, daughter of (the house of) Imrān, who guarded her chastity. We breathed Our spirit into her (womb), and she accepted the truth of her Lord's words and revelations, for she was among the ones who obey. [12]

☁ Think About It

1. When his wives started gossiping, how do you think the Prophet flt and why?

2. Why is it important for a family to be able to trust each other?

3. Why is punishment sometimes terms as "being repaid?"

4. What is the role of repentance, or asking for forgiveness, in the daily life of a sincere believer?

5. Choose one of the women mentioned in verses 10-12. Who did you choose, and what is the lesson of her example?

Fill in the Words on the lines below.
Look at the **BOLD** words in the main text to see where they go
Words to Use
Light   Confidence   Repaid   Promises

1. *"Our Lord, perfect our _____ and forgive us, for You have power over all things."*

2. Allah has already given you a required method to cancel your (hasty) _____.

3. When the Prophet told something in _____ to one wife, she told it to another, and Allah made this known to him.

4. *You're not being punished as much as you're being _____ for what you did!"*

Complete the Crossword Puzzle Below

(Words can be in any direction, even backwards!)

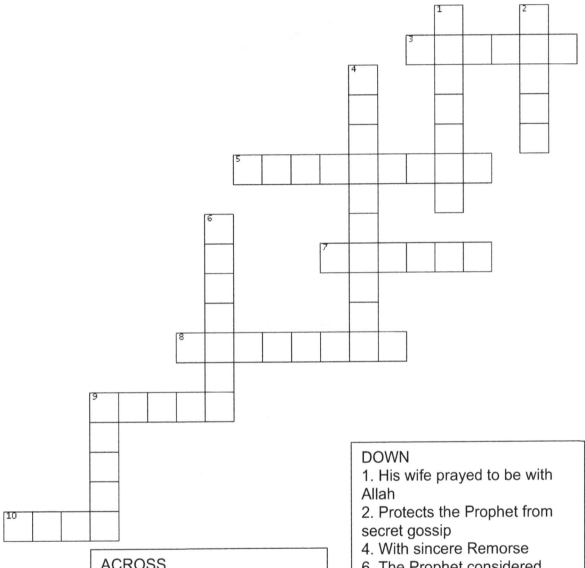

DOWN
1. His wife prayed to be with Allah
2. Protects the Prophet from secret gossip
4. With sincere Remorse
6. The Prophet considered doing this
9. It will be there before them and their right hands

ACROSS
3. Allah will do this on Judgment Day for the believers
5. Allah is the
7. The mother of 'Esa
8. There is a method to cancel hasty ones
9. Idols are made from this
10. One told another a secret

Arabic Text

بِسْمِ اللَّهِ الرَّحْمَٰنِ الرَّحِيمِ

١ يَا أَيُّهَا النَّبِيُّ لِمَ تُحَرِّمُ مَا أَحَلَّ اللَّهُ لَكَ تَبْتَغِي مَرْضَاتَ أَزْوَاجِكَ وَاللَّهُ غَفُورٌ رَحِيمٌ

٢ قَدْ فَرَضَ اللَّهُ لَكُمْ تَحِلَّةَ أَيْمَانِكُمْ وَاللَّهُ مَوْلَاكُمْ وَهُوَ الْعَلِيمُ الْحَكِيمُ

٣ وَإِذْ أَسَرَّ النَّبِيُّ إِلَىٰ بَعْضِ أَزْوَاجِهِ حَدِيثًا فَلَمَّا نَبَّأَتْ بِهِ وَأَظْهَرَهُ اللَّهُ عَلَيْهِ عَرَّفَ بَعْضَهُ وَأَعْرَضَ عَنْ بَعْضٍ فَلَمَّا نَبَّأَهَا بِهِ قَالَتْ مَنْ أَنْبَأَكَ هَٰذَا قَالَ نَبَّأَنِيَ الْعَلِيمُ الْخَبِيرُ

٤ إِنْ تَتُوبَا إِلَى اللَّهِ فَقَدْ صَغَتْ قُلُوبُكُمَا وَإِنْ تَظَاهَرَا عَلَيْهِ فَإِنَّ اللَّهَ هُوَ مَوْلَاهُ وَجِبْرِيلُ وَصَالِحُ الْمُؤْمِنِينَ وَالْمَلَائِكَةُ بَعْدَ ذَٰلِكَ ظَهِيرٌ

٥ عَسَىٰ رَبُّهُ إِنْ طَلَّقَكُنَّ أَنْ يُبْدِلَهُ أَزْوَاجًا خَيْرًا مِنْكُنَّ مُسْلِمَاتٍ مُؤْمِنَاتٍ قَانِتَاتٍ تَائِبَاتٍ عَابِدَاتٍ سَائِحَاتٍ ثَيِّبَاتٍ وَأَبْكَارًا

٦ يَا أَيُّهَا الَّذِينَ آمَنُوا قُوا أَنْفُسَكُمْ وَأَهْلِيكُمْ نَارًا وَقُودُهَا النَّاسُ وَالْحِجَارَةُ عَلَيْهَا مَلَائِكَةٌ غِلَاظٌ شِدَادٌ لَا يَعْصُونَ اللَّهَ مَا أَمَرَهُمْ وَيَفْعَلُونَ مَا يُؤْمَرُونَ

٧ يَا أَيُّهَا الَّذِينَ كَفَرُوا لَا تَعْتَذِرُوا الْيَوْمَ ۖ إِنَّمَا تُجْزَوْنَ مَا كُنْتُمْ تَعْمَلُونَ

٨ يَا أَيُّهَا الَّذِينَ آمَنُوا تُوبُوا إِلَى اللهِ تَوْبَةً نَصُوحًا عَسَىٰ رَبُّكُمْ أَنْ يُكَفِّرَ عَنْكُمْ سَيِّئَاتِكُمْ وَيُدْخِلَكُمْ جَنَّاتٍ تَجْرِي مِنْ تَحْتِهَا الْأَنْهَارُ يَوْمَ لَا يُخْزِي اللهُ النَّبِيَّ وَالَّذِينَ آمَنُوا مَعَهُ ۖ نُورُهُمْ يَسْعَىٰ بَيْنَ أَيْدِيهِمْ وَبِأَيْمَانِهِمْ يَقُولُونَ رَبَّنَا أَتْمِمْ لَنَا نُورَنَا وَاغْفِرْ لَنَا ۖ إِنَّكَ عَلَىٰ كُلِّ شَيْءٍ قَدِيرٌ

٩ يَا أَيُّهَا النَّبِيُّ جَاهِدِ الْكُفَّارَ وَالْمُنَافِقِينَ وَاغْلُظْ عَلَيْهِمْ ۚ وَمَأْوَاهُمْ جَهَنَّمُ ۖ وَبِئْسَ الْمَصِيرُ

١٠ ضَرَبَ اللهُ مَثَلًا لِلَّذِينَ كَفَرُوا امْرَأَتَ نُوحٍ وَامْرَأَتَ لُوطٍ ۖ كَانَتَا تَحْتَ عَبْدَيْنِ مِنْ عِبَادِنَا صَالِحَيْنِ فَخَانَتَاهُمَا فَلَمْ يُغْنِيَا عَنْهُمَا مِنَ اللهِ شَيْئًا وَقِيلَ ادْخُلَا النَّارَ مَعَ الدَّاخِلِينَ

١١ وَضَرَبَ اللهُ مَثَلًا لِلَّذِينَ آمَنُوا امْرَأَتَ فِرْعَوْنَ إِذْ قَالَتْ رَبِّ ابْنِ لِي عِنْدَكَ بَيْتًا فِي الْجَنَّةِ وَنَجِّنِي مِنْ فِرْعَوْنَ وَعَمَلِهِ وَنَجِّنِي مِنَ الْقَوْمِ الظَّالِمِينَ

١٢ وَمَرْيَمَ ابْنَتَ عِمْرَانَ الَّتِي أَحْصَنَتْ فَرْجَهَا فَنَفَخْنَا فِيهِ مِنْ رُوحِنَا وَصَدَّقَتْ بِكَلِمَاتِ رَبِّهَا وَكُتُبِهِ وَكَانَتْ مِنَ الْقَانِتِينَ

Surah 66 Transliteration

Bismillahir Rahmanir Rahim

1. Yaa ayyuhan nabiyyu lima tuharrimu maa ahallal laahu laka tab taghee mardaata az waajik; wallaahu ghafoorur raheem

2. Qad faradal laahu lakum tahillata aymaanikum; wallaahu mawlaakum wa huwal 'aleemul hakeem

3. Wa iz asarran nabiyyu ilaa ba'di azwaajihee hadeethan falammaa nabba at bihee wa azharahul laahu 'alayhi 'arrafa ba'dahoo wa a'rada 'am ba'din falammaa nabba ahaa bihee qaalat man amba aka haaza qaala nabba aniyal 'aleemul khabeer

4. In tatoobaa ilallaahi faqad saghat quloo bukumaa wa in tazaaharaa 'alayhi fa innal laaha huwa mawlaahu wa jibreelu wa saalihul mu'mineen; wal malaa'ikatu ba'dazaalika zaheer

5. 'Asaa rabbuhoo in tallaqakunna aiy yubdilahoo azwaajan khairam minkunna muslimaatim mu-minaatin qaanitaatin taa-ibaatin 'aabidaatin saa-ihaatin saiyibaatin wa abkaaraa

6. Yaa ayyuhal lazeena aamanoo qoo anfusakum wa ahleekum naaran waqoodu han naasu wal hijaaratu 'alayhaa malaa'ikatun ghilaazun shidaadul laa ya'soonal laaha maa amarahum wa yaf'aloona maa yu'maroon

7. Yaa ayyuhal lazeena kafaroo la ta'tazirul yawma innamaa tujzawna maa kuntum ta'maloon

8. Yaa ayyuhal lazeena aamanoo tooboo ilal laahi tawbatan nasoohan 'asaa rabbukum aiy yukaffira 'ankum sayyi aatikum wa yud khilakum jannaatin tajree min tahtihal anhaaru yawma laa yukhzil laahun nabiyya wallazeena aamanoo ma'ahoo nooruhum yas'aa bayna aydeehim wa bi aymaanihim. Yaqooloona rabbanaa atmim lanaa nooranaa waghfir lana. Innaka 'alaa kulli shay-in qadeer

9. Yaa ayyuhan nabiyyu jaahidil kuffaara wal munaa-fiqeena waghluz 'alayhim; wa ma-waahum jahannamu wa bi-sal maser

10. Darabal laahu mathalal lillazeena kafarum ra ata Noohin wamra-ata Loot. Kaanataa tahta 'abdayni min 'ibaadinaa saalihayni fakhaanata ahumaa falam yughniyaa 'anhumaa minal laahi shai-an wa qeelad khulan naara ma'ad Daakhileen

121

11. Wa darabal laahu mathalal lil lezeena aamanumra ata Fir'awn; iz qaalat rab bibni lee 'indaka baytan fil jannati wa najjinee min Fir'awna wa 'amalihee wa najjinee minal qawmiz zaalimeen

12. Wa Maryama banata 'Imraanal latee ah sanat farjahaa fana fakhnaa feehee mir roohinaa wa saddaqat bi kalimaati Rabbiha wa Kutubihee wakaanati minal qawniteen

Now You are Ready to Move On to the Next Book

Juz Tabarak

Part 29 of the Holy Qur'an

Selected Other Books for Kids by Yahiya Emerick

Visit: www.amirahpublishing.com to see the latest books!

Layla Deen and the Case of the Ramadan Rogue
By Yahiya Emerick

Somebody's trying to ruin her Ramadan! Layla Deen and her family were just settling in to break a long days fast when their mother came running from the kitchen and cried, "*Someone stole the food for Iftar!*" Layla knew it was a terrible crime and decided to get to the bottom of this mystery. See what happens! Illustrated. Ages 8-16.

Ahmad Deen and the Curse of the Aztec Warrior
By Yahiya Emerick

Where is he? Ahmad Deen and his sister Layla thought they were getting a nice vacation in tropical Mexico. But what they're really going to get is a hair-raising race against time to save their father from becoming the next victim of an ancient, bloody ritual! How can Ahmad save his father and deal with his bratty sister at the same time? To make matters worse, no one seems to want to help them find the mysterious lost city that may hold the key to their father's whereabouts. And then there's that jungle guide with the strangely familiar jacket. Are they brave enough—or crazy enough, to take on the Curse of the Aztec Warrior? Illustrated. Ages 8-16.

Ahmad Deen and the Jinn at Shaolin
By Yahiya Emerick

A once in a lifetime chance! Ahmad Deen is one of ten lucky students in his school who gets an all-expense paid trip to China. But instead of *getting* a history lesson, Ahmad may become a victim *of* history as he is thrust in the middle of a bizarre web of superstition, corruption and ancient hatreds that seek to destroy all who interfere. Who kidnapped his room-mate? What clue can only be found in the Shaolin Temple? How will Ahmad learn the Kung-Fu skills he'll need to defeat the powers of darkness. or will he fall prey to the mysterious *Jinn at Shaolin?* Illustrated. Ages 9-16.

Layla Deen and the Popularity Contest
By Yahiya Emerick

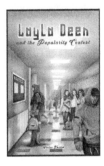

Layla is in junior high now, and she has found it hard to adjust. Friends seem in short supply so Layla becomes quiet and withdrawn. Then a school popularity contest throws her world into a tailspin. Find out what happens. Ages 9-16.

Isabella: A Girl of Muslim Spain
By Yahiya Emerick

A classic tale about a young girl who finds Islam, and danger, amidst the harrowing religious conflicts of medieval Muslim Spain. Experience firsthand what life was like in the splendid Muslim city of Cordoba. See through the eyes of Isabella as she struggles with her father's beliefs and finds that life is not always as easy as people think. Embark on a journey into history, into the heart, as you follow her path from darkness into light. Illustrated. Ages 10+

The Seafaring Beggar and Other Tales
By Yahiya Emerick

A delightful collection of short stories, poems, essays and other writings that showcase a variety of themes and inspirational nuggets of wisdom. Many of these stories and poems have been published in international magazines and are sure to put a smile on your face and a warmth in your heart for the beauty that is Islam. Illustrated. Ages 10+

Qur'an

The Meaning of the Holy Qur'an for School Children
Compiled by Yahiya Emerick

For the first time ever we now have a complete translation of the entire Qur'an into kid-friendly English. Complete with simple line drawings and background information – this is indispensable for the home and your children. For grades 4-7.

126

A Journey through the Holy Qur'an
Presented by Yahiya Emerick

An easy to read translation with the reasons for revelation interspersed throughout the text so that the Qur'an and its background can be better understood. Ages 14 - adult.

The Holy Qur'an in Today's English
Presented by Yahiya Emerick

This book contains the main text of the Qur'an with reasons for revelation at the bottom of each page in footnote format. It contains other commentary and resources, as well. Great for personal study and inspirational reading. Ages 16 - adult.

The Holy Qur'an: As If You Were There
Presented by Yahiya Emerick

This is a translation of the Holy Qur'an meant for teenagers. It has all the reasons for revelation that explain the background of the verses. It also has lots of thiking questions and great explanations for the menaing of different verses and concepts. Ages 12 - adult.

See more at:

www.amirahpublishing.com

127

Made in the USA
Middletown, DE
23 April 2023

29352153R00073